NEGOTIATE
PERSUADE
AND CREATE
GREAT DEALS

NEGOTIATE
PERSUADE
AND CREATE
GREAT DEALS

Michael Benoliel
Geetanjali Mukherjee
Jose Yong

 **World Scientific**

NEW JERSEY · LONDON · SINGAPORE · BEIJING · SHANGHAI · HONG KONG · TAIPEI · CHENNAI · TOKYO

Published by

World Scientific Publishing Co. Pte. Ltd.

5 Toh Tuck Link, Singapore 596224

USA office: 27 Warren Street, Suite 401-402, Hackensack, NJ 07601

UK office: 57 Shelton Street, Covent Garden, London WC2H 9HE

British Library Cataloguing-in-Publication Data
A catalogue record for this book is available from the British Library.

NEGOTIATE, PERSUADE AND CREATE GREAT DEALS

ISBN 978-981-122-541-3 (hardcover)
ISBN 978-981-122-542-0 (ebook for institutions)
ISBN 978-981-122-543-7 (ebook for individuals)

For any available supplementary material, please visit
https://www.worldscientific.com/worldscibooks/10.1142/11969#t=suppl

Desk Editor: Sandhya Venkatesh

Typeset by Stallion Press
Email: enquiries@stallionpress.com

Printed in Singapore

CONTENTS

ABOUT THE AUTHORS

Michael Benoliel

Michael Benoliel is the author and editor of several books, book chapters, and articles on negotiation and influence. He received his doctorate degree from George Washington University in Washington, D.C., and was trained in Negotiation and Leadership in the Program on Negotiation, Harvard Law School, and in the Participant Centered Model at the Harvard Business School. As an international trainer, he has delivered executive development workshops on negotiation and influence to Hewlett-Packard (in Sydney, Tokyo, Singapore, and Kuala Lumpur), Mitsubishi, Fuji-Xerox, British Petroleum, Shell Oil, Turkish Airlines, Caterpillar, Advanced Micro Devices, Pfizer Pharmaceutical, Henkel AG (in South Korea), Zuellig Pharma, Mega Lifesciences (in Thailand), BATA Shoes, Prudential, Keppel; Ernst Young, The Adani Group, ZS Associates, Project Management Institute (in New-York, Pittsburgh, Hong Kong, and Singapore), Accor; Singapore Stock Exchange, Mekong Capital ,(Vietnam); Indian Railways, and Indian Oil. After teaching at the Johns Hopkins University and University of Maryland University College, he joined the business school at the Singapore Management University (SMU) from 2007 to 2017. Among his many teaching awards are: Most Outstanding Faculty Award, Executive Master of Business Administration (EMBA) Class of 2015;

Mind Opener, MBA Class of 2015; Appreciation in Years to Come Award for making a difference in students' professional lives in 5 years' time, MBA Class of 2014; Outstanding Faculty Award, EMBA Class of 2013; the Most Outstanding Faculty Award, EMBA Class of 2012; Innovative Teacher Award 2010; and Dean's Teaching Honor List in 2009, 2010, and 2014. Some of Professor Benoliel's media interviews include: *ABC News*; *Bloomberg Television*; *Reuters*; *The Straits Times*; *The Washington Diplomat*; and *The Wall Street Radio*. Currently he is affiliated with Duke CE, North Carolina; Executive Education at the Singapore Management University (SMU); and the Center for Executive Education at the Indian School of Business. Professor Benoliel lives in Potomac, Maryland, USA and manages the Center for Negotiation. Contact: mbenoliel@centerfornegotiation.com or mbenoliel@aol.com.

Geetanjali Mukherjee

Geetanjali Mukherjee grew up in India, spent her early years in Kolkata, and then attended high school in New Delhi. She went on to read law as an undergraduate at the University of Warwick, United Kingdom, where she specialised in international law. Subsequently, Geetanjali earned a Masters in Public Administration from Cornell University, USA. She is a recipient of the Everett Public Service Fellowship and a member of Pi Alpha Alpha, the Global Honor Society for Public Affairs and Administration. Geetanjali currently works as a risk consultant for Fortune 500 clients in Asia Pacific. She is the author of nine non-fiction books and currently lives in Singapore.

Dr. Jose Yong

Dr. Jose Yong is a social psychologist who studies the evolved motives that underlie human psychology and behavior. His research draws from Dobzhansky's insight that "nothing in biology makes sense except in light of evolution". Likewise, a better understanding of the human mind can be achieved by uncovering what it was designed, through evolutionarily selective forces, to do. His work spans a wide range of substantive topics including relationships, motivation, organizational behavior, well-being, and sustainability and has been published in internationally renowned outlets such as American Psychologist, Journal of Personality and Social Psychology, Psychological Science, and Personality and Individual Differences.

INTRODUCTION

Based on personal interviews with more than 25 world-class master negotiators in business (e.g., Robert Johnson, founder and former Chairman of Black Entertainment Television, and Kenneth J. Novack, former Vice Chairman of Time Warner), in politics (e.g., James Baker, former Secretary of State and former Senators Bill Bradley and Robert Dole), in law (e.g., Kenneth Fienberg, Special Master of the Federal Victims Compensation Fund of September 11, 2001 attacks and Lloyd Cutler, former White House Counsel), in sports (e.g., Leigh Steinberg and Jeff Moorad, super sports agents); in diplomacy (e.g., Shimon Peres, former President of Israel, Dr. Sa'eb Erakat, Chief Palestinian Negotiator, Ambassador Charlene Barshefsky, former US Trade Representative, and Ambassador Dennis Ross, former US Envoy to the Middle East), and in labor (e.g., Richard Trumka, President of AFL-CIO and Morton Bahr, former President of Communication Workers of America), we identify and explore the best negotiation practices of master negotiators. To get a global perspective on masterful negotiation, master negotiators in business, politics, diplomacy, and law in Singapore, India, Thailand, and Indonesia were also interviewed.

Throughout the book, we give numerous accounts of the attitudes, tactics, and strategies of the interviewed master negotiators and others. For example, James Baker never underestimates the value of masterful preparation and planning. He always adheres to the rule of 5P's taught to him by his father: "Prior Preparation Prevents Poor Performance". Ambassador Charlene Barshefsky suggests that negotiators have to persuade the other side to trust them not just by words, but by the way they go about the negotiation. She also suggests that their approach must be strategic: "You must think and act strategically," she said, "by examining your options and selecting the moves that are most advantageous in enhancing your overall goal." Having an idea but no money to fund it, Robert Johnson recounted how he pitched an investment in Black Entertainment Television and suggested that negotiators must invest in building a social network: "Make your friends before you need them," he advised. In the context of time pressure and using time strategically, Leigh Steinberg said, "It is often not until there is true pressure that people reveal their final position." When it comes to setting priorities, Richard Trumka suggests that negotiators must differentiate between their 'needs' — the essential interests that they must have in order to come to an agreement, and their 'wants', which is a wish list — the interests they would like to have. Shimon Peres talked about the difference between tactical and strategic negotiators. Tactical negotiators, he said, are interested in scoring points and winning the battle. Strategic negotiators, in contrast, are willing to forgo short-term gains in order to protect their long-term interests. As a result, he said, they are anticipatory, likening them to hunters: "A good hunter doesn't aim at the bird. If he does, he will miss. He aims ahead of the bird, anticipating its travel."

We also describe and draw important lessons of negotiation best practices and effective strategies from published negotiations. For example, the negotiation between Dwight Manley, who represented the eccentric and erratic basketball player Dennis Rodman, and Jerry Krause, the Chicago Bulls general manager. The gap between the parties was large and the stalemate was long. Still, using creative deal-design, the two parties came together and agreed on a satisfactory contract that incorporated both their interests.

Although there are many great lessons to be learned from the experiences of the interviewed master negotiators and other nego-tiation events in the real world, this book is not just about 'negotia-tion war stories', however interesting. In order to ensure that this book provides practical suggestions that negotiators can use, we include many relevant concepts and principles of negotiation, and discuss how they can be applied. For example, in Chapter 6 on negotiation styles and strategy, we describe different negotiation styles and provide specific guidelines on how to respond to nego-tiators who are more interested in win-lose outcomes than in cre-ating mutual value or win-win outcomes. In Chapter 4 on influence, we specify a number of persuasion strategies, such as reciprocity, scarcity, and authority, and how to use them. In the context of making offers and counteroffers, we introduce the principle of *anchoring* and suggest how to use it in certain cases, and how to avoid being trapped by it in other cases.

The field of negotiation is dynamic and is rapidly becoming more interdisciplinary. Therefore, to keep up with the latest research, we have also included three unique chapters on deception, human evolution, and neuroscience. In short, the book, although not meant to be an academic textbook, is a balanced blend of practice and theory.

***

Master negotiators possess four main capitals or skillsets — cogni-tive capital, emotional capital, relational capital, and cultural capi-tal. In Chapter 1, we detail these four capitals. Cognitive capital refers to the ability to understand and analyze the substantive issues in a negotiation. Emotional capital alludes to the ability of the negotiator to perceive and regulate their emotions during the course of the negotiation. Relational capital enables the negotiator to build trust and develop relationships with their counterparts in order to improve negotiation outcomes. Negotiators who possess cultural capital are able to effectively navigate the nuances of different cultures and operate effectively in complex cultural contexts. These four skillsets are multifaceted, but they can be developed in order to succeed at the complex task of negotiation.

Successful negotiators behave and think differently from unsuccessful ones, and in Chapter 2, we share nine principles of effective negotiation and influence that separate master negotiators from their counterparts. These principles include doing your homework, managing the structure and processes of the negotiation, being resilient and creative, and being willing to walk away from bad deals.

Chapter 3 deals with power in the context of negotiation. Power is the capacity to influence others to get what you want by altering the perceptions, preferences, or opinions of your counterparts. Power in the context of negotiation can come from knowledge, relevant expertise, as well as relationships. Often we assume that the party with less power in a negotiation is at a distinct disadvantage, but there are ways to increase your power and improve your negotiation outcomes. In addition, we explore some hardball tactics employed by negotiators and how to respond effectively.

Influence and persuasion are at the heart of negotiation, and yet influencing another person is one of the hardest skills of social interaction. In Chapter 4, we discuss the prerequisites of influence, and unexpected but effective tactics of influence such as incremental change, reciprocity, and social proof. We also teach you to use your senses as well as non-verbal communication to succeed at influencing your counterpart.

In Chapter 5, we explore the mechanics of building trust with your counterpart. When negotiators trust each other, they share more information, develop alternatives, and creatively design outcomes that benefit all parties. However, humans evolved to be suspicious of strangers and building trust, particularly across cultures and contexts, can be tricky. In this chapter, we discuss the nature and foundations of trust, how to build trust, and how to restore violated trust in negotiations.

In Chapter 6, we discuss negotiation styles and appropriate strategies for each style. Negotiators primarily pursue win-lose (competitive), win-win (cooperative), or a combination of outcomes. Depending on your own negotiation style, there are different techniques to deal with those who create value versus those who prefer to claim value. We also describe how to focus on interests and not simply on positions.

When negotiations fail, companies end up with significant financial losses and countries are unable to make peace. In Chapter 7, we consider the cognitive biases that lead to negotiators making poor and costly decisions. For instance, one such factor is confirmation bias, which leads negotiators to pay attention to information that confirms their preconceived beliefs while ignoring data that runs counter to that belief. We also show how framing an issue and anchoring, amongst others, can impact price and negotiation options in subtle but crucial ways.

It is very common in today's world for negotiating parties to come from different cultures, even from opposite sides of the world. In

Chapter 8, we discuss the influence of culture on negotiation, and explore the cultural roots and worldview of negotiators from India and China, two rapidly growing economies. We also detail the main differences of communication styles, approaches to relationships, and notions of fairness, among others, between Asian and Western negotiators.

Lying can be extremely beneficial in negotiations, and the other party has a strong incentive to lie to get more from the deal. In Chapter 9, we describe the types of lies you may face in a negotiation, how to detect whether your counterpart is lying, and tactics to prevent or minimize deception by your counterpart.

In Chapter 10 on human evolution and negotiation, we demonstrate how certain traits transmitted from the ancestral environment still influence negotiators' behaviors, for example, the innate trait to trust your close family and social network, and distrust strangers. *Mate selection* is another important aspect of human evolution, with high risks and costs of failing to mate with the right partner. Similarly, we highlight situations when organizations 'mate' (in joint ventures or mergers) or when individual negotiators 'mate' (negotiate) with the wrong partner and experience challenges, including death, i.e. business bankruptcy.

In Chapter 11 on neuroscience and negotiation, we describe the latest research in brain science as it relates to how the brain influences the attitudes and behaviors of negotiators. For example, the role of *loss aversion*, patterns of decision making, emotions, empathy, and fairness in negotiation. For example, an experiment monitoring the brain scans of people playing fairness games, known also as ultimatum games, revealed that people tended to feel less empathy toward individuals who played unfairly. The research therefore suggests a link between fairness and empathy that has direct implications for negotiation. Not only is it suggested that fair play and cooperation promote feelings of trust and empathy, just *observing* selfish and uncooperative behavior prompts negative emotions, such as anger and a desire to punish non-cooperators.

Organizations that wish to succeed at the negotiation task need to build a culture and ecosystem that supports negotiation excellence. In Chapter 12, we describe the structures and processes that form part of a negotiation ecosystem, as well as the four stages of development of an organization's negotiation capabilities. Finally, we provide suggestions for building individual and organizational negotiation competencies.

Chapter 1

THE NEGOTIATOR'S FOUR CAPITALS

In 1716, Francois de Callieres, a French diplomat wrote, "The art of negotiation with princes is so important that the fate of the greatest states often depends upon the good or bad conduct of negotiations and upon the degree of capacity the negotiators employed." This sound advice is still largely ignored because, as Leigh Steinberg said, "Most people enter a negotiation virtually unarmed and make the mistake of negotiating before they are ready. They have done little or no preparation and have a vague, often arbitrary, notion of what they want and march forward. They are not properly prepared to get the results they are seeking, and so they rarely get those results."

Not surprisingly, academic studies have shown that about 70% of all large corporate deals fail to create meaningful shareholder value. And yet, the negotiation task, unlike other important tasks like marketing or supply chain management, remains unstructured, sporadic, often improvised, and rarely analyzed critically in the post-deal stage. This is the *negotiation paradox* — that a task which can create enormous value for corporations and individuals is so de-valued.

Why do individuals and organizations not sufficiently appreciate the value that negotiation can create? There are four main reasons.

Firstly, many believe, however falsely, that the ability to negotiate and influence people is an innate, natural-born skill — either you have it or you do not. Until very recently, most Japanese organizations, for example, did not offer training in negotiation, believing that it cannot be taught. A major Japanese conglomerate, operating internationally, has only recently started to offer negotiation workshops to its employees. In the US and elsewhere as well, countless professionals negotiate on a regular basis without any training in negotiation and influence.

Secondly, many deal-makers suffer from the *illusion of competency*. They believe that they already know how to create good deals. For example, in 1999, the consulting firm KPMG found that 83% of corporate mergers failed to create value. When the managers of the acquiring companies were interviewed, 82% of them rated their acquisitions as successful. Clearly, while individuals themselves overestimate their ability, they are consistently failing to create the required value for their organizations.

Thirdly, negotiators and organizations underestimate the price of negotiation malpractice and fail to create good deals. This happens because, in the real world, it is not always easy to measure how much value is left on the table by a marginally competent negotiator. In a training program, however, it is easy to see how much value negotiators fail to capture and leave on the table.

Fourthly, the reason that explains the negotiation paradox phenomena is the lack of organizational support. A negotiator's performance is dependent on his or her knowledge, skills, and experience. However, this is not enough. More value can be created when negotiators have a supporting environment or ecosystem. More specifically, a set of norms, processes, and structures that are designed to support the negotiator's performance. Can you imagine a highly competent pilot flying from one city to another without the support of ground personnel and the guidance of air traffic control? Similarly, how can negotiators "fly" without organizational support and still be expected to produce good results? High-performing organizations, such as Google or Apple Computers, are successful for many reasons. One of the reasons for their success is the combination of well-trained professionals supported by an organizational ecosystem.

Negotiation capital should be considered from two levels — individual and organizational. At the individual level, a negotiator needs to master four capitals, namely cognitive, emotional, relational, and cultural. At the organizational level, organizations must create an ecosystem of norms, processes, and structures that are specifically designed to support their negotiators' performance. This chapter focuses on the negotiator's four capitals of negotiation. Chapter 12 in this book is devoted entirely to identifying the components of an organization ecosystem and how to build organizational negotiation capabilities.

Cognitive Capital

In the bitter fight for control of Paramount Pictures, a global producer and distributor of films, in 1993 between former media conglomerate Viacom's Chairman Sumner Redstone and Barry Diller, the chairman of the QVC Network, Diller rushed to beat out Redstone by being the first to announce a tender offer — a proposal to buy Paramount's stock directly from the stockholders. Under a tender offer, there is a 20-day period in which stockholders can sell their stocks to the party making the offer. When a party gets 50.1% of the stock, a sale is declared, and that party becomes the controlling owner of the company, in this case Paramount Pictures. What Barry Diller did not realize, however, was that a tender offer only becomes official when the legal papers and finances are in order. Sumner Redstone, who anticipated Diller's move, made sure his legal papers were in order and his finances were lined up. Then, as soon as Redstone heard about Diller's offer to the stockholders, he filed all the appropriate legal papers and announced his competitive tender offer. Because Diller had not studied the procedure adequately, he had to spend two extra days filing legal papers, while Redstone was already purchasing stocks from the stockholders. Redstone credits Diller's knowledge-gap and the time lapse for his victory in taking over Paramount Pictures.

Cognitive capital refers to the inherent value in the negotiator's ability to understand, analyze, and synthesize the substance or the issues of the negotiation. More specifically, it is the ability to reason, plan, solve problems, think abstractly, comprehend complex ideas, learn quickly, and learn from experience. Cognitive capital is particularly important in complex negotiations that require managing a vast amount of information, designing a negotiation strategy, formulating bundled trade-offs, creating multiple proposals and analyzing complex counter-proposals, and making rational decisions. Cognitive ability is also important in ambiguous situations that present either risks or opportunities. When a proposed deal is based on the future performance of a product or a person, it has to be estimated as future performance is uncertain, and that is always risky.

Take a hypothetical scenario — imagine that you are a business agent negotiating on behalf of your client, in this case, a rising movie star. When the movie star was still relatively unknown and at the start of her career, you negotiated only one issue — her fixed salary. But now this single-issue contract is no longer enough. To capitalize on her star power in the next contract negotiation for a new movie, you want to negotiate three issues: (1) a fixed salary; (2) a bonus if she wins an acting award for the upcoming movie; and (3) a percentage of the movie's future revenues from merchandizing sales, which will vary based on whether or not she wins an acting award for the upcoming film. This situation requires a higher level of cognitive ability.

Research has shown that cognitive capital plays an important role in negotiation. It was found that there is a strong link between a negotiators' cognitive capital and their ability to create win-win agreements. Moreover, cognitive ability is a good predictor of a negotiators' ability to reach integrative or win-win agreements.

Emotional Capital

Emotional capital refers to the value inherent in the negotiator's ability to perceive, comprehend, analyze, and regulate emotions in the face of emotional challenges in negotiation. The challenge you face as a negotiator primarily is how to manage your negative emotions, such as anxiety, stress, fear, or frustration, that are triggered by the inherent uncertainty and risk in any negotiation situation. One source of uncertainty, for example, is the unpredictable behavior of your negotiating counterparty, who may use threats, deception, or even delay tactics.

Research has shown that emotions influence the behavior of negotiators, as well as the negotiation's process and outcomes. Positive emotions, for example, help negotiators reach agreements and build future relationships, foster flexibility in problem solving, increase mutual concession making, decrease hostile behaviors, and contribute towards building trust.

Interestingly, about 300 years ago, Francois de Callieres recognized the role of emotions, especially the impact of negative emotions on negotiation. At the time, he wrote that a man (or a woman) who is naturally violent and easily carried away by emotions is ill-fitted for the conduct of negotiation. Such a negotiator is ill-equipped as a successful negotiator because he or she is unable to manage their emotions constructively. Ask yourself the question: Do you manage your emotions constructively or do your emotions manage you?

Professor Baba Shiv, a neuro-behaviorist and expert in decision-making, argues that individuals do not make pure rational decisions that are free from the interference of emotions. He has shown that individuals whose 'emotional brain' (the limbic brain) has suffered damage, cannot make decisions. Decisions, therefore, spring from two sources — the rational brain (the neo-cortex) and the emotional brain (the limbic brain). Daniel Goleman popularized the concept of emotional intelligence and defined it as "the extent to which a person is attuned to his or her own feelings and to the feelings of others." Emotional intelligence includes the qualities of self-awareness, self-regulation, self-motivation, patience, and empathy.

Self-awareness. Self-awareness means being cognizant of your own thoughts, moods, impulses, and behaviors, and being aware of how they affect you and those with whom you are negotiating. For example, the chairman of the 1996 Northern Ireland peace talks, former Senate Majority Leader George Mitchell demonstrated the ability to look inward, connect to his emotions, and manage them well. After meeting for a year and a half and listening for hundreds of hours to the same arguments, he looked inward and reflected on his feelings. "I felt frustrated and angry," he wrote. "I worked hard not to let my anger show...I was very angry and considered letting it all out," he continued, because he thought "perhaps an emotional outburst would shock them all." But, Mitchell concluded, "It was too late. Nothing I said now could produce an agreement...I had to look to the future. Once again, I would have to be upbeat."

Self-regulation. Self-regulation does not imply masking all of one's feelings; on the contrary, it refers to channeling one's emotions into behavior that is appropriate to the situation. Thus, self-regulation should be understood as mastering one's emotions so that one can repress extreme anger when it is important to do so, while at the same time being able to convey it when it is strategically necessary.

James Baker, the former US Secretary of State, recounts how his negotiations with Hafez al-Assad, the former President of Syria, were grueling, protracted, exasperating, and often emotional. Most of the time, Baker was able to monitor and regulate his strong emotions very well. For example, in one session, Baker was furious when Assad suddenly re-opened issues for negotiation that he had previously assured Baker were a done deal. Baker consciously modulated his irritation and referred to Assad's calculated reversal as a misunderstanding, thereby side-stepping a potential landmine.

At the same time, when Baker felt a display of emotion might advance the negotiating agenda, he deliberately expressed his anger. In the midst of one particularly frustrating session with Assad, which had lasted nine hours and forty-five minutes without a break, Baker intentionally slammed his briefcase shut with some force to let the Syrian leader know how angry he was. Baker's rare theatrical drama was the result of emotional exhaustion brought on by a long and frustrating effort to finalize a deal. In this instance, Baker used drama to send a signal as to how far the other side could push. The action was especially effective because it was so uncharacteristic of him.

Self-motivation. Self-motivation is the quality that enables individuals to pursue their goals with persistence and energy in the face of difficulties and frustrations, and to maintain a laser-like focus on what they want to achieve.

Studies of Olympic athletes, world-class musicians, and chess grand masters show that they all share a common trait: the ability to push themselves and rise above difficulties and disappointments. In politics, many point to President Jimmy Carter's self-motivation as the central force behind the extraordinary success of the 1978 summit between Israel and Egypt, which resulted in the historic Camp David Accord. President Carter displayed not only a command of the substantive issues and impressive social skills during the two weeks of the summit, he also showed that he had stamina. In one of the most intense episodes of negotiation between Prime Minister Menachem Begin of Israel and President Anwar el-Sadat of Egypt, Carter's faith, optimism, and dogged determination pushed him to creatively find compromises where others might have relented.

Self-motivation may be difficult to maintain in high-stakes negotiations, especially when they are between parties who have been involved in a decade-long protracted and violent conflict. However, Shimon Peres, the former president of Israel, had commented that the changing relationship between Egypt, Jordan, and Israel has taught him to remain an optimist and move forward, believing that what was impossible yesterday is possible today, and what is impossible today will be possible tomorrow. "I am an optimist," he said, "and when I get a 'no' as an answer, I am not angry. I don't lose my patience. I don't lose my persistence."

Patience. Effective negotiators know that wide gaps between parties take time to narrow and close. In labor-management negotiations, the give-and-take can be protracted and the desired goal may take a long time to be achieved. As the President of the American Federation of Labor and Congress of Industrial

Organizations (AFL-CIO), the largest federation of unions in the United States, Richard Trumka said, "You just keep working your way through that." It is the virtue of patience that propels you. "If you expect to come and have everything fall into place in two hours and then go to dinner," Trumka said, "then probably, you are not suited to be a negotiator. Sometimes it takes weeks, sometimes longer — months and years."

In the case of the Panama Canal, it took 14 years to negotiate the Panama Canal treaty. In the case of the Korean War in the 1950s, it took 2 years and 575 meetings to negotiate an end to this war. "You can't go into negotiations and expect a very rapid resolution of differences," former President Gerald Ford said, adding, "The differences are often very valid. They require gradual movement."

Washington lawyer and master mediator, Kenneth Feinberg, defines a master negotiator as someone who is flexible, persistent, creative, and optimistic. Optimism, Feinberg says, is important "because no matter how difficult the disputed gap between the parties might be, if one maintains an optimistic view that reasonable people can reach an accommodation, that optimism goads you forward."

On the first day of the mediation over compensation to the US Vietnam veterans for their exposure to Agent Orange (a toxic chemical that was sprayed from the air over North Vietnam by the United States military during the Vietnam War), Feinberg asked the lawyers representing the US Vietnam veterans how much money they wanted. Their response: US$1.2 billion. "I then turned to the chemical companies, Dow and Monsanto," Feinberg says, "and I asked them what they were willing to pay in response to this demand. Together, they said, they would pay $25,000." It took a lot of optimism, persistence, time, and patience to close this gap.

Empathy. Empathy is the fifth component of emotional intelligence. It builds on self-awareness and can be defined as the propensity to understand the feelings of others and take their views into account when formulating trade-offs and offers. Empathy also refers to the ability to read emotions via verbal messages and non-verbal cues, such as a person's tone of voice, gestures, and facial expressions. It is, as Robert Johnson, the founder of Black Entertainment Television (BET) points out, "the ability to read the [negotiation] room."

Palestinian Chief Negotiator Sa'eb Erakat believes respect is a stepping stone to empathy. He advises, "Respect the other side. Don't ever undermine his or her concerns. Try to understand his or her point of view, whether you agree or disagree with it. Try to feel what the other side is feeling."

Every year on the evening of Holocaust Memorial Day, a siren sounds all over Israel for two minutes as a mark of remembrance, and all activities come to a halt. Traffic stops and people stand silent. Erakat has lived under Israeli occupation for 50 years, ever since he was a boy of 12. Nonetheless, he says, when he was negotiating with the Israelis in Tel-Aviv on one such day, he stood up silently beside the Israeli negotiators when the siren went off.

Clearly, negotiators who have emotional capital — self-awareness, self-regulation, self-motivation, patience, and empathy — are much better able to manage negative and positive emotions constructively and keep the negotiation moving forward.

Relational Capital

Negotiation, at its core, is relational between people first and negotiators second. Relational capital refers to the inherent value in the negotiator's ability to develop relationships, nurture trust, show respect, be flexible, play fair, and build a positive reputation over time.

Research has shown that relational capital leads to improved interactions with counterparties and, most importantly, to improving the negotiation's outcomes. Specifically, relational capital contributes to greater information sharing, increases solidarity and reciprocal behavior, encourages the parties to search for creative solutions in the face of potential impasse, and focuses the negotiators on win-win negotiation.

Effective negotiators, like James Baker, former US Secretary of State, believe that relational capital can facilitate even the most contentious issues in negotiation and resolve them. Ambassador Dennis Ross, who had worked with James Baker, said that the relationship between the parties is the "sine-qua-non": more important than anything else. "People," he said, "will reveal things to you because of the relationship you have with them." For example, he added, they will help you to negotiate more effectively by pointing out that certain calculations which you have made about trade-offs are, in fact, incorrect.

Whether in business or politics, your relational capital will help you move forward your agenda. For instance, legislators who are interested in having their political agendas supported by other legislators routinely socialize with them, said former Senator Bill Bradley. "In the Senate, there are informal gatherings of senators. There are cloakrooms where you have informal discussions. There are family events where spouses come. There are trips that you take where you spend days with colleagues," Bradley said. "All of these help to create good relationships with your colleagues, as opposed to being off on your own and operating pretty much in a blind. I have done that, and I learned. I think it's an important lesson."

Ehud Barak, the former Israeli Defense Forces Chief of Staff and the most decorated Israeli soldier, did not appreciate the future value that comes from investing in building relationships and trust. After a long military career, he moved to politics and became the Prime Minister of Israel for a short period of time, from 1999 to 2001. During the Israeli-Palestinian negotiation in July 2000 in Camp David, Barak displayed a cold and dismissive attitude towards the late Yasser Arafat, the former Chairman of the Palestinian Authority. For days, Barak remained reclusive in his cabin while Madeline Albright, the former US Secretary of State, and Barak's own team repeatedly encouraged him to spend some informal time with Arafat and build a relationship with him. But Barak remained dismissive. "Socializing and eating baklava (a Mediterranean pastry) with Arafat," Barak said, "would not change anything." For Barak, the negotiation was about the disputed issues and not about relationships. This attitude on Barak's part had a negative impact on the negotiation.

Effective negotiators, whether in politics or in business, would suggest otherwise. Eric Benhamou, CEO and Chairman of 3Com, for example, invests in building relational capital. Specifically, he said, "When I know that I am negotiating with someone that I need to do business with over a long period of time, obviously I will try to build a relationship and avoid a confrontational style, avoid burning bridges."

An important element of relational capital is the negotiator's reputation. A historical example is the relationship between banker Pierpont Morgan and steel mogul Andrew Carnegie in the late 19th century. In 1873 when the financial market was in great panic and many companies were going bankrupt, Carnegie found himself pressed for funds to pay his financial obligations. He had invested $50,000 in a partnership interest with Pierpont Morgan that he figured had increased in value about $10,000 since the initial investment. So, he asked Pierpont to return $60,000 to him. Instead, Pierpont gave him a check for $70,000, explaining that the investment had actually generated $20,000 in profit, not $10,000. In his autobiography, Carnegie wrote that because of this exchange, he would never harm the Morgans.

Robert Johnson concurs. "It is important for me to have the currency of a good reputation," he said. "Being candid, honest and forthright about my intentions generates future opportunities for doing business, because the more you are like that [trustworthy], the more your counterparts are going to come to you with deals because they know they are going to get honest answers."

Cultural Capital

When former US Ambassador to the United Nations, Jeanne Kirkpatrick, asked the foreign ministers of the Association of Southeast Asian Nations (ASEAN) countries if there were good prospects for settling the Cambodian-Vietnamese armed conflict in the late 1970s and 1980s, they all said, "Yes." And when she asked, "Do you think it will be very soon?" They all said, "Oh yes, very soon." "Well, how soon?" she wanted to know. "Oh, about five years' time," they said. She was shocked. She was thinking in months while they were thinking in years.

Time, which is fundamentally a natural phenomenon and exists everywhere in the universe, is a cultural factor that has different cultural, social, and psychological meanings in different cultures. As such, it influences negotiators' behaviors, the negotiation process, and the negotiation outcomes. Not surprisingly, time and pace are common topics in negotiation training.

Cultural dimensions such as time, tolerance for uncertainty, how relationships are built, the expression of emotions, pattern of communication, and others, make cross-cultural negotiations complex and affect the negotiation process and outcomes. For example, negotiations between Japanese and American individuals produce sub-optimal agreements because they don't know the rules of engagement in the other culture and the best way to navigate through the thick cultural fog of global negotiation. Take for example an information exchange between American and Japanese negotiators. The process can be very long because Japanese negotiators are risk-averse, play it safe, and move slowly because they ask many questions and require an enormous amount of information before they can begin to negotiate. American negotiators, in contrast, move faster because they are more risk-seeking, ask fewer questions, and require less information at the start of the negotiation process.

Tommy Koh, Ambassador-at-Large and former Ambassador of Singapore to the United Nations, is a highly respected international negotiator and mediator. Commenting on cultural differences in negotiation, he said, "I am always astonished by the fact that ministries of foreign affairs pay so little attention to historians and cultural anthropologists." When he was asked to mediate an international dispute between European parties, he took a significant amount of time off from his duties at the Singapore Ministry of Foreign Affairs in order to study the histories and cultures of the parties. It is when you know the culture of your negotiating counterparty that you can better understand why they behave in a certain way.

Cultural capital refers to the inherent value in the negotiator's ability to understand the stated and unstated values, norms, practices, and nuances of different cultures, and negotiate effectively in complex cultural contexts. Armand Hammer, the former CEO of

Occidental Petroleum, demonstrated cultural sensitivity and used his cultural capital well. When he presented his bid to get a Libyan oil concession, it was written on a sheepskin parchment, rolled up, and tied with green and black ribbons (the Libyan national colors). To the Libyans, Hammer had demonstrated that he was familiar with their culture and respected it. He won the oil concession.

Research in cross-cultural negotiation has shown that the negotiator's level of cultural capital predicts their effectiveness in cross-cultural situations, as well as their engagement in information-seeking behaviors which foster integrative solutions. Cultural capital promotes convergence between different ways of thinking (holistic versus specific), contributes to developing relationships and trust over time, and minimizes negative interpretations of motivations and behaviors.

Building cultural capital is even more important for those of us involved in the global economy. When working with negotiators from different countries and cultural backgrounds, it is even more important to acquire a deep understanding of the different cultural dimensions, which may include: the degree to which the culture is individualistic or collectivistic, the degree to which power is held by the few or the many within the country, whether the communication style of the counterparty is direct or indirect, the degree to which individuals in that culture are risk-averse or risk-seeking, the degree to which people display emotions in public, the role of time, the degree of formality or informality, the degree to which negotiators invest in building relationships, how trust is built, the nature of contracts, attitude towards space, and value of human dignity ('saving face').

Motivated negotiators can develop cultural capital by exploring the visible and invisible values and practices within that culture.

A simple approach is to identify differences and understand the sociological, psychological, theological, and historical reasons that explain these differences. For example, why do some westerners, like the Italians and French, display emotions openly and comfortably in public while some easterners, like the Singaporeans and Japanese, refrain from displaying emotions in public? In the chapter on cultural negotiations, a number of cultural dimensions will be identified and discussed, including suggestions for developing cultural capital.

As the negotiation task is complex, negotiators need to have mastery of all these four capitals — cognitive, emotional, relational, and cultural. It is only when negotiators have all these assets that they will be able to manage information and make complex decisions, manage their emotions constructively rather than being managed by their emotions, build authentic and trusting relationships, and interact competently with negotiators from different culture. Fortunately, with effort and perseverance, all these four capitals are skills that can be learned.

Chapter 2

PRINCIPLES OF MASTERFUL NEGOTIATION

Master negotiators use a combination of attitudes, knowledge, and skills that can be categorized into nine principles of effective negotiation and influence. In this chapter, we list and discuss these principles and use examples to demonstrate how these principles can be applied in a variety of negotiation situations. These principles are not listed in a particular order of importance.

Be Prepared to Walk Away from a Bad Deal

Electronic Data Systems (EDS), the world's second-largest computer services company in the late 1990s, competed with IBM and others in 2000 to win a large US Navy and Marine Corps contract. During the fierce competition, EDS, which was favored to win the contract, slashed its original bid of $8.6 billion by $1.7 billion and also agreed to stiff conditions for payment, such as deferring payments for equipment and salaries until performance standards and targets were met and approved by the Navy.

EDS won the deal — the largest multi-billion-dollar computer outsourcing contract on record that was designed to merge 400,000 of the US Navy and Marine Corps' decades-old computers in more than 1000 disparate networks into one Web-based Intranet.

Once EDS started to work on this contract however, it found 100,000 different software applications on these computers — a much larger number than the company had anticipated — and hundreds of old applications that could not be moved to the new system, requiring many workers to still juggle two computers on their desks. Two and a half years later, EDS found itself well behind schedule. After almost three years, EDS had invested hundreds of millions of dollars in this contract and had yet to receive a single penny from the Navy. Three weeks before he stepped down, EDS CEO Richard H. Brown admitted the experience had taught the company some hard lessons. By the end of the first quarter of 2003, EDS was reporting substantial losses on a contract that had cost it $334 million.

Negotiators are prone to making mistakes, including two specific decision mistakes. First, by rejecting a deal that should have been accepted. Second, accepting a deal that should have been rejected. The question, therefore, is: Why do negotiators accept offers that they should have rejected, and make deals that should have never been made? There are several reasons.

First, the deal-making process is not costless. It always requires human and capital resources. When negotiators fail to make a deal, these costs are not salvageable and become sunk-costs. Negotiators, not surprisingly, dislike to lose and let go of sunk-costs. Faced with the prospect of no-deal, which implies failing to create positive value and creating negative value in the short term, negotiators who lack discipline and favor short-term gains opt for making a deal. Effective negotiators, on the other hand, know that letting go of sunk-costs, as painful as it is, is better than entering into a bad deal that will be costlier in the future.

Second, negotiators who are facing the possibility of no-deal, although justified, tend to feel that they personally failed in the negotiation task because their task, they believed, was to make a deal. But that is incorrect. The negotiator's task is **to only make good deals**. To counter the feeling of failing to make a deal, negotiators should frame the situation correctly and say: *This is a bad deal that should not be made. I am only concerned with making good deals!*

Third, when you, as a negotiator, represent an organization, you are always concerned with your reputation and success. Justifiably, you might be concerned that failing to make a deal might affect your organizational reputation as a deal-maker. However, effective negotiators would suggest that here again you should frame the situation correctly. If there is no-deal, you should suggest that it was justified and say: *I saved the organization from a bad deal!*

Fourth, the reason for entering into bad deals is the negotiator's self-interest. Robert Kohlhepp, the former vice chairman and former CEO of Cintas, suggested that negotiators rush to close deals because they are evaluated and compensated based on the number of deals they close. When organizations reward deal-makers for closing deals, it should not be surprising that self-interested deal-makers are more motivated to make deals than not.

Effective negotiators are aware of the bias to make deals and not to walk away. Thus, they condition themselves to walk away from a deal, if necessary. For example, in the acquisition of Keebler Company, a producer of cookies and crackers, that Carlos Gutierrez, former CEO of Kellogg, the cereal conglomerate, desperately wanted, he mentally conditioned himself that he might not get it. He offered a price, committed to it, and was prepared to walk away from the deal. This commitment, Gutierrez said, "helped me to stand firm on a price." He got his deal.

The decision of whether to make a deal or walk away from it should be based on clear guidelines. Joe Trustey, the partner at Summit Partners, a private equity investment firm, is guided by the following four guidelines: First, the objectives of the deal must be clear. Second, the proposed deal must be subjected to a test against the deal's objectives. Third, the deal-maker should not be emotionally tied to the deal. Fourth, the negotiators should not be desperate to make the deal because there will be other opportunities in the future. Comparing Summit Partners to other corporations, Trustey said, "We are less emotionally tied to the deal than many corporate buyers. If we miss this deal, we know that we'll get the next one."

The decision whether to make a deal or walk away from it is a critical moment, or as Sumner Redstone described it, a moment of no-return, which negotiators have to be prepared for: "You have to be prepared to walk. If the price is too high, you walk away." Reflecting on the negotiation process to acquire Paramount Pictures, Redstone recalled, "We were not going to do a deal at any cost. We were going to do it only if it made sense. We were prepared to walk away." Robert Johnson, similar to Gutierrez, Trustey, and Redstone, suggested that in every deal there are things that are so important to the success of the business that if he can't get them, there is no point in making a deal. So, when he negotiated a new joint venture with a young music artist, he was clear on what he needed, stayed focused on his interests, and was disciplined throughout. The music artist, failing to consider Johnson's no-deal option, insisted that Johnson, a multi-billionaire, forgo future investment opportunities in other music record label companies, and invest only in their joint venture — a music record label. Johnson boldly refused and this is how he described that moment and exchange in the interview:

> I was putting up all the money and giving him [the music artist] a controlling interest in the business. I had to have the right to

invest in other record companies, if I wanted. I have huge amounts of money in other business interests and there is no way that you can expect me to say that I will never invest in another record label, just in yours. Well, the music artist said that if I retain the right to do that, then I have to give him the right to buy me out when I do that. I am not going to give you that right, I told him, and if you are going to insist on that, then go and find three million dollars from somebody else. There is not going to be a deal.

Johnson, firm, disciplined, and with a good measure of empathy, softened his punch and skillfully de-escalated the situation. "Look," Johnson told the artist, "I have no intention of investing in another record label company. I like you. Why do you think I came to you? But I just can't give you that kind of control over my business interests." They made the deal.

Take the Other Side's Perspective

"The secret of negotiation," wrote Francois de Callieres, "is to harmonize the interests of the parties concerned." To harmonize different interests, effective negotiators negotiate from both sides of the table by 'traveling mentally' from one side of the table to the other. In this process, they hope to discover the other side's interests, priorities, aspirations, capabilities, and limitations. The genuine discovery of the other side's mind-set is possible only by doing what is called *taking the other side's perspective*. It is the capacity to understand your counterparty's point of view and thereby predict their strategies and tactics.

Taking the other side's perspective, however, is neither natural nor easy since we are accustomed to seeing the world from our own lenses. Or as former US Secretary of State James Baker said, "Many negotiators are self-centered. They are so preoccupied with what they need and want, they pay much less attention to what the other side needs and wants." And our self-centered perspective, according to former US Supreme Court Justice Louis D. Brandeis, is the source of costly conflicts. He said, "Nine-tenths of the serious controversies which arise in life result from one man not knowing the facts which to the other man seem important, or otherwise failing to appreciate his point of view."

Take, for example, the unfortunate case of Robert McNamara, former US Secretary of Defense who served under President John F. Kennedy and Lyndon B. Johnson, who was in charge of the Vietnam War in the late 1960s and early 1970s. Throughout the war, McNamara was committed to escalating its costs, which led to the loss of more than one million North Vietnamese soldiers and civilians, and billions of dollars in material, even when it appeared that the war was unwinnable. It would take him several decades to learn the principle of taking the perspective of the other side.

In the documentary film titled *The Fog of War* released in 2003, Robert McNamara admitted that the United States never understood the North Vietnamese well enough to comprehend their motivation to sacrifice more than one million soldiers and civilians. From the American point of view, the war was part of the Cold War — a fight against the spread of communism. For the North Vietnamese, the war was about liberation from nearly 100 years of oppressive Western colonialism. "You were fighting to enslave us," a former Vietnamese minister told McNamara decades after the war. The minister continued, "We were fighting for our independence...and had you understood our history, you would have realized that we were not pawns of the Chinese and the Soviets [Communists]. We fought the Chinese for 1000 years — fighting for our independence — and for this reason, we were determined to fight to the last man. No amount of US bombing would have stopped us." (The American bombing in Indochina amounted to 7.66 million tons of explosives, compared to 2.15 million tons in World War II.)

In retrospect and much regret, McNamara suggested that we must try to put ourselves inside the skin of the other side and look at ourselves through their eyes in order to understand the way they think, and what lies behind their decisions and actions.

Research has shown that negotiators who take the perspective of the other side are better able to promote emotional connections, nurture trust, and produce superior outcomes than negotiators with lower perspective-taking ability. To develop this ability, negotiators should learn from individuals in the intelligence community. In a private meeting with Yaakov Perry, the former head of the Israeli Shin Beth (internal intelligence agency), he was asked, "What did you learn from your personal experience of combating terrorism in the last 30 years?" Perry immediately replied, "Do not hate your enemies, the terrorists. If you do," Perry explained, "you will not be able to understand how they think, what makes them tick or how they recruit others."

Negotiators can use two techniques to develop a perspective-taking ability. One is *role reversal*. It is used by some lawyers when they prepare for trials. A defense attorney, for example, will reverse their role, and role-play a prosecutor. Role reversal can be used by negotiators in a mock negotiation practice. For example, if you are a seller, reverse your role to a buyer. Specifically, focus on the other side's cognitive and emotional states by imagining how the other side thinks and feels.

The second and complementary technique is *interactivity*. It is not enough to read about and imagine how the other side thinks and feels, and role play it. Studies have shown that true understanding of the other side comes from on-going discovery — asking questions and listening to their concerns and circumstances during the negotiation process.

Be Resilient and Creative

Research has shown that inexperienced negotiators tend to give up prematurely and leave the table without a deal, although there is good value to be created. Effective negotiators, in contrast, are resilient and creative. They continuously look for creative ideas that might bridge their differences because they know that deal-making is not easy, especially when negotiators have critically important interests.

In sports, said Leigh Steinberg, "Carmen A. Policy, the former President and CEO of the Cleveland Browns football team, has a critical quality — resilience. He has the ability to come back from the most frustrating negotiation situations, which seem so complex that there is no way that they will ever be resolved. And yet, he comes back with a fresh approach to fight another day."

Another sports example is the case of Dennis Rodman, the flamboyant and eccentric basketball player who played for the Chicago Bulls. He was a talented sports star but difficult to manage. Rodman regularly missed many games due to disciplinary problems, including a suspension of 11 games for kicking a courtside cameraman in the groin. Dwight Manley, Rodman's agent, represented him in the contract negotiation with the Chicago Bulls in the summer of 1997. Rodman, aware of his star power, demanded a high salary of $10 million for the following season, which was one million dollars more than his previous one-year contract. On the other side of the table was Jerry Krause, the Chicago Bulls' general manager, who was reluctant to spend such a large amount of money on an unpredictable player. But Krause's situation was not easy because he had pressure from the Bulls' fans and from Michael 'Air' Jordan — the best basketball player in the world — who had publicly demanded that the Bulls re-sign Rodman for the upcoming season.

The salary gap between what Dwight Manley asked for and the amount that Jerry Krause was prepared to offer was wide, and despite the pressure to make a deal, an impasse was imminent. At that moment, what was needed to bring about a successful deal was not just resiliency, but also creativity. After a long stalemate, Manley and Krause designed a contingent contract that included a low base salary and defined incentives, which rewarded Rodman for each game he took part in. Ultimately, Rodman received approximately the amount he had originally demanded and the Chicago Bulls also got what it wanted, namely a dependable and cooperative star that played 80 regular season games for the first time in six years!

Creativity is a critical quality that negotiators need, said Eric Benhamou, especially when in a deadlocked negotiation. Such situations, he said, "leave you with the most satisfaction. Just when you thought you were headed to a brick wall, toward a no-deal, some other angle is revealed, and you find a way to accomplish your objectives and also meet the objectives of the other side without giving up much." Therefore, negotiators, especially in difficult situations, should neither give up prematurely nor press the other side too hard. Instead, they should be creative.

Let's go to the early stage of the Internet and see how Microsoft designed a creative deal. Two years after Netscape, a competitor, released its impressive web browser, Navigator, in 1994, it became the dominant player in the industry with 80% share of the market.

To Microsoft, this was a serious competitive threat. "If there were ever a bullet with Microsoft's name on it," a senior executive from Microsoft said then, "Navigator is it. "

A year later, in August 1995, Microsoft released its own web browser, Internet Explorer, which was bundled free with Windows. By then, America Online (AOL), one of the first Internet service providers, was already booming with more than five million existing customers and 250,000 new ones joining every month. When Microsoft's chairman, Bill Gates, pitched Microsoft's browser to AOL's chairman, Steve Case, he was rebuffed. However, Bill Gates was resilient and creative because Microsoft simply couldn't afford to lose the browser war to Netscape. Microsoft designed a creative deal that played well to its overall strengths and to AOL's needs, rather than just focusing on price and their browser's technical prowess. Specifically, Microsoft offered to give the Internet Explorer browser free to AOL, to integrate it seamlessly into AOL's software, and to place the AOL icon on the Windows desktop — "the most valuable desktop real estate in the world." It was a creative knockout that destroyed Netscape's market value.

Since resilient and creative negotiators create superior deals, how can you develop these capabilities? First, to be resilient is to be patient with the long process of change because negotiators almost always resist change, especially a big change. Negotiators prefer to move towards each other in small steps, in effect accepting incremental change. From this perspective, the negotiation itself is a ripening process where you are making your counterpart ready to take the long journey toward saying yes. The second factor is the mind-set of *mastery*. In the face of challenges, negotiators who have a strong sense of mastery, i.e. the ability to influence the situation and the outcomes, are more likely to remain in the negotiation situation and influence it patiently.

In terms of applying creativity to deal-making, there are a number of ways to create creative deals. You should identify the full set of interests of the other side and carefully disclose your interests, build on compatible interests that you can easily agree to, do logrolling or trade-off between interests, use contingent contracts that bridge the difference between negotiators' time preference (short- versus long-term) or risk tolerance (low- versus high-risk), design flexible packages that fit the parties interests, and in a case of team-on-team negotiation, create a heterogeneous team that is able to think and approach the negotiation from diverse viewpoints.

Do Not Issue Ultimatums

When Sumner Redstone was pursuing the acquisition of Paramount Pictures, he was short on cash and needed more money to do the deal. To get more money, one option was to merge Viacom with Blockbusters, the video rental company, that at the time had excellent cash flow. Another option was to do a deal with BellSouth, the telephone company. John Clendenin, the CEO of BellSouth, together with Bruce Wasserstein of the investment banking firm Wasserstein, Perella & Company, were prepared to invest billions of dollars, much more than Redstone really needed. In a meeting with Redstone, Clendenin announced that in return for his investment, he wanted 50% of the deal. Initially, Redstone assumed Clendenin was referring to 50% of the Paramount deal. However, as Clendenin clarified, he wanted 50% of Redstone's company, Viacom International (which includes Paramount as well as Viacom's other existing business units). If this offer was not outrageous enough, Clendenin added a threat. "If you will back out on this proposed deal," Clendenin told Redstone, "I will go to Barry Diller (who was bidding against Redstone to also acquire Paramount)." When Clendenin asked Redstone for his response to this offer, Redstone just walked out of the room.

Not all effective negotiators respond to threats and ultimatums in the same way. Ambassador Charlene Barshefsky, faced with an ultimatum, neither confronts the counterparty negotiator nor leaves the room. She ignores it and uses humor to diffuse its destructive power. Richard Trumka also does not let threats escalate the negotiation situation and throw him off track. "[If] somebody makes a threat or gives me an ultimatum," he said, "I just look at him or her. I just continue the negotiation process." Although effective negotiators deal with threats and ultimatums differently, they have a common approach — diffuse them.

Negotiators use ultimatums in order to pressure the other side to comply with certain demands. Usually the demand includes a set deadline for compliance, and implied or explicit threats of punishment for non-compliance. Often, inexperienced negotiators, frustrated with the negotiation process, use threats and ultimatums too casually. Most of them, however, fail. One reason is that the target (the receiver) of the ultimatum does not perceive it as credible and believes that the issuer of the ultimatum will not follow up with the threats. This was the case in Iraq's invasion of Kuwait in 1990. US President, George H. Bush, issued an ultimatum to Iraqi President Saddam Hussein, demanding compliance with UN Security Council Resolution 678 to leave Kuwait. Bush's demand was accompanied with a threat: "You, the Ba'ath Party, and your country will pay a terrible price." Saddam dismissed the threat as not credible. The credibility test has to do with the perception of the recipient of the ultimatum and not the issuer. In other instances, ultimatums fail because the target perceives the ultimatum as credible but is still willing to defy it because the benefits of defiance are greater than the costs of compliance. For ultimatums to be successful, they must be perceived by the targets as *credible and too costly to defy.*

Sometimes, 'fake ultimatums' work well because negotiators who receive them tend to focus on their own potential costs of defiance and ignore the potential costs to the other side who issued the ultimatum. For example, imagine that after a long negotiation, you are finally ready to sign the contract but suddenly there is an add-on in the last minute. Your counterpart says, "To sign this contract we need another concession, otherwise there is no deal." What would you do? Most negotiators get stressed and give in because they think more about their own possible costs and less of the possible costs to the other side if there is no-deal. Walking away from a deal in the last minute is very difficult for any negotiator because it always involves costs. Furthermore, important issues and interests are not introduced in the very last minute.

Although most ultimatums fail, effective negotiators sometimes cautiously use them because they are necessary. When the negotiators on the other side are not negotiating in good faith and delay the negotiation process, Leigh Steinberg suggests that an ultimatum can be used to focus the parties to bring a lingering situation to a resolution. "In our business [sports and entertainment]," he said, "everybody does everything in the last second. So, it is not until there is true pressure that people reveal their final positions...So, whether it is an imminent [sports] training camp or an artificial deadline, the key is that both parties believe it, act upon it, and shape their behavior in a way where they really get down to the bottom line."

Create Mutual Value

"If you want to win, go to war, don't negotiate," Shimon Peres suggested. "Negotiations," for him, "are about finding an accommodation that both sides can live with. When you negotiate, don't think only in terms of what you can win — more concessions and victories you can bring home — but also what the other side can win, so that they too can claim some achievements."

In a rare television interview, Efraim Halevy, the former chief of the Mossad (the Israeli intelligence service), recounted how a major crisis with Jordan was managed. In mid-September 1997, a group of Mossad agents infiltrated Jordan, and on Thursday, September 25 at 10 a.m., two Mossad operatives tailed Khaled Mashal, a top political leader of the Palestinian group Hamas, in their green Hyundai rental car. When he arrived outside his office building, a Mossad operative approached him and injected him with a poison. However, Mashal survived after receiving a life-saving antidote in time.

The two agents fled the scene but couldn't escape. They were arrested. Four other agents from the back-up team fled to the Israeli Embassy. The botched assassination triggered a serious diplomatic crisis. Jordan's King Hussein felt challenged personally. He was ready to storm the Israeli Embassy, close it down, and prepare the two captured Mossad agents for a public trial.

Most of the Israeli officials involved in trying to resolve the situation were focused entirely on how the fiasco would affect Israel and how to get out of it, with one exception. The way to manage this crisis, Efraim Halevy suggested to his colleagues, is to begin to understand the problems they had created for King Hussein and how Israel might help Hussein resolve these problems.

Halevy, known for his gentle manners, wide connections with Arab leaders, and deep understanding of the Arab culture, went on a secret mission to see the King of Jordan. He agreed to accept the King's demand that Israel release Sheik Ahmed Yassin, the founder and spiritual leader of Hamas, and dozens of other Hamas prisoners. He intentionally did not negotiate nor demand a quid pro quo — the release of the Israelis in return. To do so, Halevy knew, would anger King Hussein. Instead, he asked the King to commit a monarch's act of compassion. The King asked him what a monarch's act of compassion was. Halevy responded that as a mere human, he was not qualified to instruct a king. King Hussein understood. He ordered the release of the Israelis. Halevy's strategy was to resolve a crisis by understanding the interests of both parties and creating mutual value.

The natural tendency of human beings, especially in crises, is to examine all problems and issues from our own point of view and create a calculated 'mental balance sheet' that reflects our own potential benefits and losses. This self-interested mindset often results in distorting or ignoring the interests of the other side. Effective negotiators know that creating mutual value is in their own best interest, for the following reasons.

Firstly, negotiators, in most cases, are independent parties who come to a negotiation freely and can walk away freely. They are not obligated to accept a bad deal or any deal. Secondly, negotiators are also interdependent on each other and a deal will happen only when all the parties say *yes* to a proposal. Thus, it must be good enough for all parties. Thirdly, a negotiated deal that ends up with an agreement, which is an exchange of promises, is just the beginning of the relationship. The next and often most important phase is the implementation of the agreement. There is always a risk that a dissatisfied party may not fulfill all its obligations, or even try to re-negotiate the deal. Fourthly, your reputation is your shadow and will always follow you. Finally, cultivating a reputation of being a value-creating negotiator will create new opportunities in the future because most people like to negotiate with value-creating and not value-claiming negotiators. Thus, it is in the negotiators' best interest to negotiate a mutually beneficial deal that is also satisfactory.

However, creating mutual value is possible only when the negotiators work together to create a win–win. In win-lose situations where negotiators try to claim value, effective negotiators know that their preferred value-creating style will no longer be effective. Thus, they need to be flexible enough to change their negotiation style to value-claiming in order to protect their interests. Effective negotiators therefore have a repertoire of behaviors and are flexible enough to change their negotiation style, moving situationally between creating value and claiming value when necessary.

Do Your Homework

Rawson Food Services, on the advice of Prudential-Bache, its financial advisor, paid about $40 million to acquire 43 supermarkets from Pantry Pride Enterprises, Inc. As it turned out, shortly after the deal was done, Rawson Food Services filed for bankruptcy reorganization and sued Prudential-Bache for negligence. Rawson argued in Florida state court that Pantry Pride was worth substantially less than what Rawson had paid for it. The court found Prudential-Bache guilty of negligence — failing to conduct proper due diligence — and awarded Rawson $26.3 million in punitive and compensatory damages.

Professors Robert Aiello and Michael Watkins suggest that many professionals in mergers and acquisitions, for example, have wiped out significant value of their firms' market capitalization "more through failures in due-diligence than through lapses in any other part of the deal process".

Interestingly, the value of doing your homework, adequate planning, and preparation is obvious, and yet it is one of the most frequent and common mistakes that deal-makers make. Why? First, negotiators de-value the task of doing their homework and underestimate the grave costs of showing up unprepared. Second, negotiators are prone to information availability bias where they rely too much on secondary and easily available sources of information, such as the Internet or industry reports, and not enough on primary and reliable sources of information, such as customers or suppliers who are familiar with the negotiation context. Third, many negotiators have a confirmation bias where they select information that confirms their pre-existing beliefs and preferences, and ignore information that is contradictory in any way (see chapter 7 on decision biases – why negotiators make poor decisions). Fourth, some negotiators are overconfident and underestimate the risks and overestimate the benefits of a potential deal. Fifth, many negotiators are inflicted with 'deal fever', where they are motivated by their self-interest and the reward that they expect to get from closing deals, and are less focused on getting the best possible deal. Finally, many negotiators do not get the necessary organizational support, such as having enough time, help from a research unit, having access to easy-to-use planning templates, or training in how to plan and prepare well for negotiation : (see chapter 7 on decision biases — why negotiators make poor decisions).

In contrast to the countless deals that have failed due to poor planning and preparation, a recent study based on a sample of 1,700 mergers and interviews with deal-makers found that the executives who led high-performing mergers conducted effective due-diligence. For example, executives from Bain Capital, an elite private equity firm, or Cinven, a leading European private equity firm, never fail to prepare and plan adequately, nor attempt to rush through this crucial process. At Bain Capital, for example, information is king, and the difference between primary sources and secondary sources of information is clear. John Connaughton, former managing director of Bain Capital, said that too many practitioners accept secondary data, such as industry reports and other third-party information, as being factually accurate when carrying out their due-diligence. "We at Bain Capital," he said, "throw out the secondary research and build our point of view from the bottom-up based on data from primary sources." Similarly, before Cinven acquired Odeon Cinema, it sent its own team of analysts to the field to 'hang out at the movies'. The analysts visited every cinema in the group in order to understand the company well, especially its future potential. It was a costly micro due-diligence approach that delivered later with a more accurate picture of the company's value, that helped to prevent Cinven overpaying for the company.

Master negotiators never underestimate the value of doing their homework. James Baker was taught 'the 5Ps principle' by his father — Prior Preparation Prevents Poor Performance. The 5Ps principle means mastering the details. For example, in the class action suit brought by the victims affected by Agent Orange, the herbicide used in the Vietnam War to defoliate trees, which had dire health ramifications for many Vietnam veterans, Kenneth Feinberg, the mediator of this case, had to study the epidemiological consequences of Agent Orange on the health of the Vietnam veterans.

Doing your homework is not a one-shot act. It is a continuous process. In Leigh Steinberg's case, continuous planning can sometimes be in real-time. When he negotiated with Mike Lynn of the Vikings (an American football team) over Wade Wilson's employment contract, the speaker phone was on. And when Mike made a set of arguments about the financial difficulties of the Vikings, a lawyer working for Steinberg and listening to the conversation, immediately "went upstairs, worked out a detailed set of responses, and delivered them to me [to Steinberg] just as Mike was wrapping up his point."

Preparation and planning are crucial because, like a puzzle, you will never find all the information in one place. It is investigative work that requires the collection of many pieces of information that may be scattered in many different places. As this task is critical, negotiators must be familiar with preparation and planning tools, have organizational support (a small team of data collectors), and use structured planning platforms.

Design Negotiation Structures

When architects design physical structures, they consider form and functionality. Once the structures are built, they remain fairly static for decades, and sometimes for centuries (the Leaning Tower of Pisa in Italy is more than 830 years old). Structures in negotiations, however, are configured and reconfigured by adding or subtracting structural elements. For example, adding or subtracting the number of issues from the negotiation agenda or the number of negotiators in a team negotiation.

Structural elements are important to the outcome of the negotiation, which is why negotiators, in the pre-negotiation phase, can often spend weeks and months negotiating the structure because it will affect how the process will unfold as well as the result. In the 2003 standoff between the United States and North Korea, it took many months to negotiate who the parties will be. North Korea insisted on a bilateral negotiation directly with the United States. The United States, on the other hand, insisted on a multilateral negotiation involving other countries — South Korea, Japan, China, and Russia. After months of overt threats and behind-the-scenes diplomacy, on August 1, 2003, North Korea formally announced that it agreed to multiparty negotiations and the United States also agreed to hold informal bilateral talks with North Korea within the multilateral framework.

Negotiators, as structural designers, consider structural elements flexible enough to rearrange them: the *parties* — who will participate in the negotiation; the *issues* — setting the agenda, large or small, of the issues; the *sequence of the issues* — the order and importance of the issues and when they will be negotiated; the *interests* — identifying the underlying needs and goals of all the parties; the *alternatives* — thinking of and creating alternatives before and during the negotiation; the *agreement* — determining the ripeness (readiness) of the potential deal; the *linkages* — thinking about how issues are linked and how the current negotiation might be connected to other negotiations; the *time* — how the passage of time will affect the outcomes of the negotiation; and the *location, venue, and schedule* — where the negotiations will take place and how long they will last for. These elements stay in place as long as they contribute to an effective negotiation process and outcomes. However, if they are no longer as effective as planned, they must be changed.

In a different context, take for example highly skilled basketball or soccer coaches as structural designers. They focus sharply on setting the configurations of their players — defensive or offensive — and how effective the configuration might be in achieving a win. If the configuration of the players is no longer effective, the coach will reconfigure it to be more effective. Thus, mastering structural configurations is an important strategic ability and often a game changer.

Edgar Bronfman, the former CEO and chairman of the Canadian conglomerate, Seagram Company, and the President of the World Jewish Congress, recognized the power of *structural moves* when he negotiated with the Swiss banks on the issue of compensation for Holocaust survivors whose families' assets had been held by the banks since World War II. At first, he was stonewalled by the Swiss banks. To put pressure on the Swiss banks and change the game, he rearranged the original structure of the negotiation — with the World Jewish Congress on one side and the Swiss banks on the other side. Bronfman added new parties to the negotiation environment by capitalizing on his political and business networks, and creating a powerful coalition with US pension funds in New York and California.

The Swiss banks, faced with political and financial pressure from Washington and New York, faced the threat of a potential massive divestiture of stocks by some of the biggest pension funds in New York and California. Furthermore, the pending proposed merger between Swiss Bank Corporation and UBS, a global financial services firm, was delayed because of the negative publicity of this case. Swiss Bank Corporation, for example, couldn't pass the 'character fitness' test that is required in order to operate a financial institution in New York State. The formidable pressure that Bronfman organized by capitalizing on the influence of other parties changed the attitude of the Swiss banks and brought them to the negotiating table. They settled with Bronfman and the World Jewish Congress received $1.25 billion to be distributed to the Holocaust survivors.

Manage Negotiation Processes

Managing the negotiation process skillfully can also be a game changer. Mastering this skill, however, is not easy. "How hard is it to learn the substance of the negotiation?" asked Ambassador Dennis Ross rhetorically. "You just learn it," he answered. "But, managing the negotiation process itself," he stressed, "is by far the most challenging part of negotiation." Indeed, 237 participants who went through negotiation training at the Harvard's Program on Negotiation concur with Ambassador Ross. In a self-evaluation study of eight different negotiation skills, they reported that they were far less confident in their ability to manage the negotiation process as compared to the other skills required in negotiation.

Why is managing the negotiation process difficult? Because, much like in a sports game, it is not predictable. Therefore, it has to be continuously managed, adjusted, and readjusted.

Jeff Moorad, the founder of Moorad Sports Management, and nationally known as a sports super-agent, knows the challenge of managing the flow of the negotiation process well. During the negotiation over the employment contract of Travis Lee, a baseball star, Jeff sensed a growing interest in his client from several sports teams. Refusing to call a price, Jeff recalled, "Teams would call and ask me 'What are you looking for?' I never answered that question until the eleventh hour, when we were close to making the final deal with the Arizona Diamondbacks." It wasn't until late in the process that Jeff felt comfortable naming his price for Travis Lee's contract. "It was not until the process played itself out that I ever felt comfortable naming a price. First of all, I didn't know that we were heading to $10 million. If I had been forced to name a price early on, I might have said five million dollars," he said.

Setting an imperfect process in negotiations or auctions can be costly. For example, a one-shot, either open or closed, auction does not always generate the highest benefit for the auctioneer. In a case of an open outcry auction, the auctioneer will get just slightly more than the second highest bidder. To extract more money from bidders, this is how Robert Barnes, a well-known Washington lawyer and book agent, sets the process for a book auction:

> If you are interested in acquiring the rights to the book of [famous person], please submit your offer in writing to me at my office no later than date [set date]. We would like to know as many details as possible. What rights do you wish to purchase (print, television, film)? What is the amount of the advance? What is the schedule of payments? What royalty level are you

offering? What is your monetary commitment to advertising? What bonuses, if any, do you propose? On [set date], I will call the low offeror and ask if he or she will top the high offeror. The process willcontinue for as long as necessary.

As the negotiating process is generally unpredictable and can affect the outcome, Barnes does not set a determined and rigid process. He designs a process that provides an opportunity to exhaust the bidding process and extract more value as the process moves from one round of bidding to the next, and then followed by direct negotiations with the top bidders. This combination is known as negotiauction (for a detailed discussion of negotiauction, see the book titled *Negotiauction* by Guhan Subramanian).

However, in negotiations, unlike auctions, one party cannot control how the process will unfold. It is subject to negotiation between the parties. Unfortunately, many negotiators tend to pay much more attention to the content, that is, 'what will be negotiated', and much less to the process, that is, 'how the negotiation will unfold over time'. An executive MBA student (who is a senior executive) of the first author Michael Benoliel went to negotiate in China. He decided to take another colleague with him. When they entered the negotiation room, they were shocked. On the Chinese side, there were six negotiators! By failing to negotiate a structural element, that is, 'how many will be in the room', the process was impacted negatively because a two-on-six negotiation dynamic is very different from a two-on-two negotiation dynamic.

In the acquisition of Rubbermaid by Newell, Rubbermaid gave Newell only three weeks to conduct their due-diligence. Not surprisingly, Newell did not detect many issues during the unreasonably short due-diligence period. For example, Rubbermaid, to make itself more attractive, stuffed its distribution channel and artificially increased its sales. This is essentially an example of 'perfuming the pig', or artificially making something look better than it is.

Experienced negotiators are aware of the impact of the process, and manage it as much as possible in advance, especially in tough negotiations. For 14 years, negotiations between the United States and Panama over the Panama Canal have been at an impasse because the United States was not satisfied with Panama's security guarantees and Panama was not satisfied with US assurances of Panamanian sovereignty. When lawyer-diplomat Sol Linowitz took over in 1977, he decided to split the negotiation process into two separate stages. The first stage would deal with the security issue, the second with Panamanian sovereignty. Once he was successful in getting an agreement on security, Linowitz reasoned, it would be easier to get the United States to deal with the issue of Panamanian sovereignty.

He was right. As he progressed in the two planned processes, Linowitz worked on building a coalition of support for the agreement. By resolving the security issue first, he got the backing of the US Department of Defense, the trust of Panamanians that their concern for sovereignty would soon follow, and the support of the 67 Senators he needed to ratify the treaty. After all these years of impasse, Linowitz, by redesigning the process, was successful in securing a Panama Canal Treaty in only six months' time.

Any process, including negotiation or negotiauction, has a time (temporal) dimension — beginning to end. In the examples of Moorad's negotiation and Barnes' negotiauction, time was used cleverly to generate and capitalize on competition. Another important dimension of the process is psychological and social. In all negotiations, negotiators produce and experience positive and negative emotions, deal with each other's personalities, develop constructive or destructive social norms, establish poor or excellent relationships, and develop high or low trust. Since these psychological and social processes affect the outcomes, negotiators must manage the psychosocial effectively. Unfortunately, most negotiators are not trained in understanding and managing psycho-social processes. They manage them intuitively, which is not sufficient. To be effective, negotiators must manage two processes simultaneously: The *temporal* process as the negotiation moves from one issue to the next, and the *psychosocial* process of negotiators' behaviors.

Work Towards Achieving Mastery

In most cases, to become a master is a lifelong process of learning, practice, growth, and march to perfection that requires an all-consuming attitude of sacrifice. Olympians, world-class scientists, and countless individuals who passionately want to become the very best have to make a conscious decision to do so and then put in years of effort.

While history has several examples of those who have achieved great heights simply due to natural talent, for instance Wolfgang Amadeus Mozart, the Austrian musical genius who created his first musical composition at the age of five, for most people mastery is not innate. Mastery for many artists, athletes, or negotiators comes from a commitment to hard work. In fact, some researchers even claim that Mozart wasn't a natural genius, and had worked hard over several years before beginning to compose his best work at the age of 14, almost 10 years after he first began the study of music. World class athletes, such as Michael 'Air' Jordan, the basketball star of the Chicago Bulls, show their commitment to mastery by continuing to work extremely hard even after they become successful. Jordan is famous for being the first to show up for practice and the last one to leave the basketball court. With unparalleled motivation, he spends countless hours at the gym to develop his muscles and physical strength, in addition to practicing the game.

Malcolm Gladwell, in his book titled, *Outliers*, describes the relentless driving ambition of masters like Bill Gates, the co-founder of Microsoft, and the Beatles, perhaps the most successful band in the world. Their mastery in computers or music is attributed to the principle of putting in 10,000 hours of hard work. The Beatles, for example, began to play music together in 1957. In the clubs of Liverpool, their home town, they played short sessions — only one hour long. In the clubs of Hamburg, Germany, in contrast, they had to play eight hours seven days a week. In just over a year and a half, they had performed 270 times. By the time the Beatles came to the US, in February 1962, they had seven years of experience and thousands of hours of playing music together.

Much is known about Bill Gates' post Harvard years. Not much, however, is known, about him at Lakeside middle school in Seattle. In 1968, when Bill was in eighth grade, Lakeside started a computer lab, well before many universities had computers. From that moment on, writes Gladwell, "Gates lived in the computer room."

Mozart, the Beatles, and Gates became great because they had a passion for their chosen activity. Similarly, to master the art and science of negotiation, you must have a passion to be a great negotiator. Most negotiators, unfortunately, not only do not have a passion for negotiation, based on the first author Michael Benoliel experience with thousands of students and executives, most dislike negotiation, and many, given a choice, would prefer not to negotiate at all.

Ask yourself: Do you like to negotiate? If you do, then you are far more likely to be successful at it. But if you do not, ask yourself: why? What does negotiation mean to you? How does negotiation make you feel? On a psychological level, discovering what negotiation means to you is an excellent place to start to begin to develop yourself as a skilled negotiator.

Chapter 3

POWER IN NEGOTIATION

Power is the core of negotiation.
William Quandt
The measure of a man is what he does with power.
Plato

Power is the capacity to influence others and get what you want — the slice of the pie that you prefer by altering the perceptions, preferences, or opinions of your counterparts. Power is at the center of any social interaction and determines the eventual outcome in negotiation. Thus, power must be carefully analyzed and assessed by asking several important questions: What is the nature of power? What are the dimensions of power? What gives negotiators power? How do you negotiate when you have power and when you don't? What are some common tactics used by those with power and are they effective? How do you deal with hardball tactics? In this chapter, we will address these questions.

Nature of Power

Power has two sides. The dark side of power is equated with domination, coercion, and oppression. It is associated with helping increase value for the more powerful party and destroying value for the less powerful. The other side of power is lighter, which is equated with making a difference in people's lives and empowering them to fulfill their potential. In this case, it is about using power for the greater good of families, groups, organizations, communities, and nations. Powerful people like Bill and Melinda Gates, Oprah Winfrey, and the Dalai Lama have been using their financial, inspirational, and moral power to improve the physical health, mental well-being, and quality of life of others. Power, therefore, is not inherently good or bad — it is simply an instrument that can be used for different purposes.

Political power, for instance, can be used constructively or destructively. In Singapore, for example, political power has been used in a paternalistic way to improve the citizens' well-being — in 2016, the income per capita was $52,600, one of the highest in the world. In Zimbabwe and Venezuela, in contrast, political power has been used to oppress the many, while benefiting the very few. In another example, US President John F. Kennedy used his political power to inspire a nation to go to the moon, to promote civil rights, and motivate the younger generation to volunteer for the Peace Corps. US President Richard Nixon, in contrast, used the power of his office to obstruct justice, mislead the American people by making false statements, and misuse the investigative power of the Central Intelligence Agency (CIA), the Federal Bureau of Investigation (FBI), and the Secret Service. For his illegal acts, he faced the threat of impeachment for committing high crimes and misdemeanors. Facing impeachment by Congress, he was pressured to resign in disgrace.

Dimensions of Power

Perception. Power is not what you actually have (vast financial resources, good reputation, information, or strong business, political or social networks), it is what the other side thinks you have. Power is in the eye of the beholder. As power is a matter of perception, it can be managed and manipulated in order to shape preferred perceptions. One way to shape the perceptions of power is by framing the situation. For example, in 1912, Teddy Roosevelt ran for president. To promote his candidacy, the campaign had printed three million pamphlets with his photo on the front cover. Just before distributing the pamphlets, a campaign worker discovered that each printed photo had a small line that read "Moffett Studio – Chicago," which held the copyright of the photo. Distributing the pamphlets without a copyright permission from Moffett Studio was estimated to cost the campaign three million dollars in legal liability. The campaign was faced with a dilemma — one that would potentially cost them a few million dollars.

George Perkins, the campaign manager, sent a telegram to Moffett Studio informing them that the campaign was planning to distribute pamphlets with Roosevelt's photo on the cover and asked: How much will you pay us to use your photo? The studio, without doing any in-depth research, offered to pay $250. Perkins accepted immediately. In this case, successfully re-framing the situation saved the campaign a few million dollars. Negotiators, therefore, should always ask themselves: What can the parties do to shape the perception of power?

Dynamic. Power is never static. It is in flux and changes either slightly or significantly during the negotiation process. Power dynamics are not unique to human societies. It also shifts in groups of gorillas and chimpanzees where access to resources is negotiated almost daily between alpha males and rival females. Similarly, the balance of power between negotiators can change in a variety of ways. One way is to change the structure of the negotiation by adding influential parties. For example, when Edgar Bronfman first negotiated with Swiss banks for compensation for Holocaust survivors whose families' assets had been held by the banks since World War II, the banks stonewalled, believing that they held all the cards. Their preferred option was not to negotiate with Bronfman, and so they did not. As described in chapter 2, to deal with the stonewalling by the banks, Bronfman changed the negotiation structure by adding new parties. He capitalized on his political connections, and after months of intensive lobbying of key politicians in New York and Washington, D.C., the banks faced a number of potential threats. Given the banks' worsening position, stonewalling Bronfman was no longer an attractive option. The Swiss banks, initially the powerful parties, changed their attitude — they came to the table and negotiated a $1.25 billion settlement with the World Jewish Congress. The funds were later distributed to Jewish Holocaust survivors. As power is most often dynamic, negotiators should ask: How likely is it that the balance of power between the parties might change and in what way? What actions should the parties take to change the balance of power?

Relevancy. Analyzing a negotiator's total power is not relevant because parties do not use their total arsenal of power. Instead, they use only the specific power (legal, financial, or professional connections) that is *relevant* to the situation. Well-known sports agents Leigh Steinberg and Jeff Moorad have *relevant power* because they represent some of the best athletes in baseball and football who are highly-coveted by many sports teams. Israel has nuclear power; however, it is not relevant to the Israeli-Palestinian conflict because it is inconceivable that it might ever be used. Negotiators, therefore, should ask: What power do the parties possess that is relevant to this specific situation?

Motivation. Having relevant power (legal, financial, reputation, social connections, diplomatic, military, etc.) does not mean that negotiators are always motivated to use it over a long period of time. In the Vietnam War, the North Vietnamese were motivated to fight to the last person standing because it was a war of independence (and more than one million Vietnamese died). The US, despite its enormous military power and years of inflicting enormous human casualties, was no longer motivated to 'stay in the fight' because it realized that it never had the same fighting spirit and public support the North Vietnamese had. Unable to win, the US pulled out and let North Vietnam take over South Vietnam.

A party's motivation to use its power is a matter of assessment based on signals that are sent before and during the negotiation or conflict. In a business context, for example, a pharmaceutical company with solid financial resources was interested in acquiring another pharmaceutical company. To discourage competition, it sent a strong signal that it was absolutely willing to invest enormous resources to ensure a successful acquisition. This signal indeed deterred potential competitors. Negotiators, therefore, should ask: To what extent are the parties motivated to use their power over time?

Neurological regulators. Based on their subjective perception of their power, negotiators express different behaviors. According to Professor Dacher Keltner and his colleagues, a negotiator's level of perceived power affects two neurological regulators that trigger different behaviors. Powerful negotiators exhibit *approach-related* tendencies, while powerless negotiators, in contrast, exhibit *inhibition-related* tendencies. Specifically, negotiators who feel powerful exhibit a positive mood, search for rewards in the negotiation situation, are not inhibited, and process information automatically. Negotiators who feel powerless tend to express negative emotions, pay attention to threats of all kind, are more likely to experience stress, control information processing, and express inhibited social behavior. To get a sense of your counterparty's power, ask: Does my counterpart exhibit approach-related or approach-inhibition behaviors?

What Gives Negotiators Power

Power, which in the context of negotiation is the ability to get the results you want, comes from both tangible and intangible resources. It is derived, as Francis Bacon said, from **knowledge (information)**. Negotiators who, for example, are knowledgeable about negotiation tactics, strategies, and principles will have an advantage over those who are not knowledgeable. Another source of power is **relevant expertise**. For example, negotiators who are well trained in the art and science of negotiation and have negotiation experience will outperform less experienced negotiators. Subject matter experts in a specific field (e.g., legal or financial experts in mergers and acquisitions in the banking industry) have more power than those who lack such expertise.

Power is also derived from one's ability to **reward** — provide benefits to those who need them or **punish** — apply 'pain' and sanctions. The US, for example, uses its international economic development programs to reward and punish developing countries which rely on such assistance. Power also comes from holding a **formal position**. The US, France, United Kingdom, Russia, and China are permanent members of the United Nations Security Council and enjoy a veto power, which more than 175 other UN members do not have. The United Nations, it can be said, was conceived, created, and managed as a system where a few countries dominate over the rest. In a commercial context, procurement managers have more power over suppliers.

Negotiators' power also come from having **relationships and social networks**, which give them better access to information and opportunities to exchange favors. The classic example is the Chinese *guanxi* — a social network that is based on relationships, trust, and the exchange of favors. Another source of power is a good *reputation*. Individuals who have a positive reputation have more power because they are known to be trustworthy and reliable. Doing business with them is less risky than with negotiators who have a shady or less trustworthy reputation.

Power is also derived from the context of the negotiation. The context may give you an opportunity to **build coalitions** with other parties, exercise your attractive **Best Alternative to a Negotiated Agreement (BATNA)** (getting a deal with someone else), or create sufficient **time** so that you are not pressed by a short deadline. For example, Kirk Kerkorian, the owner of Metro-Goldwyn-Mayer/United Artists (MGM/UA) studios, understood the value of time. On July 25, 1985, Kerkorian told Ted Turner, the founder of CNN, that he was going to put MGM/UA up for auction in two weeks but would give Turner the first option to buy the company. Ted Turner could buy the company for $1.5 billion, if he closed the deal in two-weeks, by August 8th. On August 6, 1985, two days before the short deadline and without any negotiation whatsoever over the price, Turner signed a purchase agreement to buy MGM/UA.

In his rush to close the deal, Turner paid $200 to $300 million more than what industry analysts thought the company was worth. He failed to notice that MGM was in a bit of a financial free-fall at the time, producing a slew of unpopular, money-losing new films. In addition, Turner's attorneys had failed to ask what recent legal commitments MGM had made, and thus did not uncover the fact that on August 4th, MGM/UA had signed a contract with Rainbow Services locking up all cable rights, and HBO had already contracted to buy several MGM movies at a very advantageous rate. Negotiators, therefore, it is important you ensure during the pre-negotiation phase that there is enough time to do adequate due diligence before you negotiate the deal.

Negotiating Without Power

Negotiating with less power than your counterpart is challenging, but doesn't necessarily mean that the party with less power will be the loser. When you are in this position, and still have to negotiate, the question you have to ask yourself is: What can I do to increase my power?

Distinct value. Power is not always related to the possession of more resources. It has to do with distinctive capability. In a personal interview, Narayan Murthy, the founder of Infosys, a global information technology (IT) company, recounted how he competed with large companies over an IT contract when his company was tiny and unknown. In a meeting with the client that was initially scheduled for two hours but ended up running to over eight hours, the client realized that Infosys, although tiny, had distinct value. Murthy won the contract.

In the classic biblical story, David, the small-framed Hebrew shepherd, and Goliath, the Philistine giant warrior, faced each other in the battlefield. To all those who had assembled to watch, the outcome of the encounter appeared predictable. Goliath was well armed with a sword, a spear, and a javelin. David, neither armed nor wearing a shield, carried only a tiny sling.

As Goliath came near, David took a smooth, round stone from his bag, put it in the sling, and shot it towards Goliath. The stone struck Goliath on his forehead, between his eyes — the only place on his body that was not shielded. Goliath fell on his face, and all the Philistines fled. Clearly, David lacked physical power but had distinctive skill that gave him a competitive advantage. The examples above indicate that you should not assume that others know your capabilities. Moreover, you should assess the weaknesses of the other side and exploit them.

Build coalitions. Effective negotiators master the art of coalition build-ing, especially when they have less power. Coalition building is designed to change the structure of the negotiation by partnering with existing parties or adding new influential parties, as Edgar Bronfman did in the negotiation with the Swiss banks. Adding parties to increase power is a classic strategy in politics and business. For example, in March 2007, ABN AMRO, a Dutch bank, announced that it was in a discussion with Barclays, a British bank, for a potential merger. Other banks, however, were also interested in ABN AMRO. Specifically, the Royal Bank of Scotland (RBS); Banco Santander, a Spanish mega-bank; and Fortis, a small Dutch bank. To compete against Barclays, they formed a consortium and created RFS Holdings for the purpose of acquiring ABN AMRO. The consortium was success-ful, and the acquisition was closed in late 2007 for about $100 billion. Note however that coalitions can be fragile as members might defect and join other coalitions when the benefits are greater. The coalitional challenge is not just in building it but also in holding it together. In the RFS Holdings case, the three banks made a pact to stay together.

Teaming and grouping purchases. Similar to the idea of building a coalition to enhance power, in the context of sales negotiation in mar-kets dominated by one or two 'players', buyers should team together and group their purchases in order to negotiate better terms.

Cut out the middleman. Thomas Stemberg, founder of Staples, in urgent need of capital to further expand Staples, went back to the venture capitalists that had initially funded him. They, however, valued Staples less than Stemberg did and thus wanted more equity in Staples, for an amount that was more than Stemberg was willing to give them. To break the power of the venture capitalists, Stemberg went to look for sources of funding elsewhere. He approached Goldman Sachs, an investment bank, but unexpect-edly, Goldman Sachs proposed exactly the same valuation as the venture capitalists. Looking for new ideas, Stemberg went to consult with Professor Bill Sahlman, who gave the suggestion to simply cut out the middleman. Specifically, he suggested that Stemberg go directly to the source of money — to the pension funds and the insurance companies who are limited partners of the venture capital firms, who often resent handing off 20% of the profits and a hefty management fee to the venture capitalists. Stemberg did as suggested and found an alternate source of funding for his firm.

Make small deals. When your attempts to increase your power throughout the negotiation fail and you still want to make a deal, then make a small deal. For example, if a multinational company is interested in your service to conduct professional training for its executives and is offering you many workshops, however at a lower price, you should resist the temptation. The suggestion is to negotiate a small deal — deliver a few workshops only. The rationale is that after delivering the workshops, your value will be fully recognized because there is a difference between knowing about you and what you can do, and actually experiencing your performance. In addition, in the process of delivering the workshops, you will have opportunities to develop connections in the company to many individuals who will also recognize your value. Once your full value is recognized, negotiate a larger deal.

Improve your alternatives. Power comes from the quantity and quality of your alternatives. But sometimes there is only one alternative and it is not attractive. That was the case in the negotiation between Malta's Prime Minister, Don Mintoff, and the British government over the rental fee of the British naval base in Malta. The Maltese Island, a strategically important British naval base during World War II, faded in significance over the decades that followed. Thus, the British government wanted to significantly reduce its rental payment to the government of Malta. Needless to say, Mintoff was displeased at the idea. Capitalizing on the Cold War division between East and West in 1971, Mintoff, faced with no alternatives, created one: He offered the Soviets an opportunity to establish a naval base on the island, and made no secret of his overture. *The Times* of London insisted that the Malta Naval Base was badly needed by Britain and should *never* be made available to the Soviets. *The Times* and public opinion pressure to eliminate the Soviet option dramatically increased Mintoff's negotiating power, and in the end, Britain's base rental payments quadrupled.

Make yourself bigger. Pufferfish, also known as blowfish, can inflate into a ball shape by filling their elastic stomachs with huge amounts of water and air in order to evade predators. The fish is in this way able to make itself look bigger than it is. People can follow the same principle. Some organizations do that by creating an impression of being larger than they are. IMD Business School, a top business school based in Switzerland, has an executive development branch in Singapore, which operates from a few offices in a high-rise building. IMD's advertising brochure, however, does not show pictures of the offices but rather a picture of the entire high-rise building. Years ago, the first author Michael Benoliel worked in a small consulting firm in Virginia, USA. The firm had a tiny service contract with the US Navy. In the advertising brochure, however, there was a picture of an entire Navy ship. Impression management works well on the ill-informed.

In negotiation, however, your counterpart knows you. Therefore, do not over-present yourself, unless you want to lose your credibility. More important than over blowing yourself, is to not feel weak and to not act small. One way to feel powerful is to mentally recall a situation where you were powerful before. In addition, act powerful by adopting power poses that project power — the way you walk, stand, sit, and hold your hands. Research has shown that individuals who adopt power poses experience hormonal changes — an increase in testosterone, which is the power hormone, and a decrease in cortisol, which is the stress hormone. Note that as long as the other side is still at the table and negotiating with you, you are not powerless.

Quit when required. One of the Chinese stratagems for weak armies is to escape. The idea is to preserve your resources rather than fight and make pointless sacrifices. Escape does not mean defeat. It means regrouping and staging a comeback at a more favorable time later. In the context of business strategy, many companies entered certain markets, did poorly, and escaped to stage a later comeback. For example, Kentucky Fried Chicken (KFC) entered the market in Hong Kong in the late 1960s, did poorly, and escaped because the market was not ready for Western fast food. Years later KFC re-entered the Asian market and is now operating in several countries across Asia Pacific. In negotiation, escaping — leaving the table and not having a deal — might be your best current strategy because no deal is better than a bad deal. Once you have more power and the timing is right, re-enter the negotiation.

Negotiating With Power

In 2006, Walmart, under a new management, decided to discontinue its relationship with Flagler Production, its video production company, and hire a more advanced high-tech video production company. This move violated a long-standing handshake deal between Walmart and Flagler Production. Consequently, Flagler had to dismiss its 16-person work force and sell its 20,000-square-foot production facility. For terminating this relationship, Walmart offered to buy Flagler's video library of 15,000 tapes. In the negotiation, Flagler asked for $150 million and Walmart's counter-offer was only $500,000. Flagler made a concession and revised its offer to $145 million. The gap was too big and a deal was never made. In response, Flagler, the legal owner of the videotapes, made the video archive available to the public, charging $250 per hour to view the videos and $1,000 per minute to screen them publicly. Some of the videos were apparently not flattering. An attorney representing a 12-year-old boy who was injured by a combustible gas canister, originally sold by Walmart, discovered a video where Walmart's managers were joking about the potential danger of the combustible gas canister. In another video, Sam Walton, the founder of Walmart, admitted that Walmart was not hiring enough women into management. In other videos there were additional embarrassing material.

Walmart, a powerful company, turned out to be overconfident in this matter. It failed to take the perspective of Flagler and evaluate its BATNA. In this case, Walmart's power in terms of market share, number of employees, or net profit was not relevant. Had Walmart better assessed Flagler's power, it would have offered more than US$500,000. Or, perhaps, it would have been more open to exploring creative solutions that might have satisfied both parties.

This case is not unusual. Powerful parties are sometimes arrogant, overestimate their power, and underestimate the power of the 'weaker' party, including the weaker party's BATNA. They are not humble enough to see the situation as the 'weak' party sees it. This was the case in the negotiation between the US and Mexico. The US believed that Mexico had no other alternatives but to sell its natural gas only to its neighbor to the north. Thus, the US negotiators offered to buy the natural gas for a low price. They did not realize that Mexico had an alternative — not to sell it at all, but to burn it instead. The US negotiators, realizing that Mexico had an alternative, improved their offer.

Powerful negotiators who negotiate with power may force the other side to give up and get what they want in the present. This approach, however, is not risk-free. Powerful negotiators, who are strategic, should consider the long-term implications for their reputation and future deals with the other party.

Hardball Tactics

300 years ago, Francois de Callieres, a French diplomat, suggested: "Menaces always do harm to negotiation because they frequently push one party to extremes to which they would not have resorted without provocation." Effective negotiators too suggest that hardball tactics, although sometimes necessary, are not effective.

Ultimatums. After Iraq invaded Kuwait, President George H. Bush ordered Saddam Hussein to evacuate Kuwait by January 15, 1991, or face the consequences. The January 15 deadline came and went and Iraq did not withdraw from Kuwait. The ultimatum failed.

Effective negotiators refrain from issuing ultimatums. When they get them, they do not respond in kind, but rather diffuse them. Former US Trade Representative Charlene Barshefsky disarms ultimatums, generally by using humor. But in one instance, she said, when her negotiating counterpart was "very aggressive, menacing almost," she didn't laugh nor tell a joke. "I sat there very quietly and did not say a word. I did not worry. I did not look upset. I did not look scared, and I did not look interested. I just had a blank expression on my face. And then, after about two minutes, he actually calmed down and we just went on as though it never happened. But, had I jumped right in and said 'How dare you?' or 'Your views are preposterous!' this would have spiraled out of control."

Kenneth Feinberg, who was appointed as a Special Master to administer the compensation funds to the victims of the 9/11 disaster in New York City, also believes in ignoring ultimatums. "You pooh-pooh it," he said. "When somebody threatens me in mediation, I urge him to withdraw the threat." In mediation, he said, it is "ill-advised ever to say 'This is my final offer. Take it or leave it.'"

There may be, however, a few rare cases where a soft ultimatum is necessary. Sports agent Leigh Steinberg said that an ultimatum can be used to force the parties to bring a lingering situation to a head. "In our business [sports and entertainment]," he said, "everybody does everything in the last second. So, it is not until there is true pressure that people reveal their final positions...So, whether it is an imminent [sports] training camp or an artificial deadline, the key is that both parties believe it, act upon it, and shape their behavior in a way where they really get down to the bottom line."

Good cop/bad cop. This is a classic tactic used in law enforcement interrogations. The dual roles create an illusion that the good cop is on your side and the bad cop is not. The reality is that neither cop is on your side.

Bill Richardson, former US Ambassador to the UN, in preparation for a meeting with Raoul Cedras, former President of Haiti, found out that Cedras liked to play the good cop and his top general, Philippe Biamby, played the bad cop. Richardson arrived to the meeting prepared. The good cop/bad cop tactic is transparent, easy to detect, and should be neutralized. First, see it for what it is: a psychological trap. Second, do not be seduced by the 'good' cop. Third, diffuse this tactic by labeling it or making it clear that you know what the other side is doing. For instance, you could say, "I see both of you are playing good cop and bad cop. It is interesting. It reminds me of a detective movie I saw last year."

Impasse. The reputation of well-known negotiators is always known because they repeat their patterns. Wayne Huizenga, former president of Blockbuster, liked to make the other side think the deal was set and final, only to pull it away, whetting the other side's appetite and making them beg him to come back. In the negotiation with Viacom's former president, Sumner Redstone, he announced suddenly, at two in the morning, that there is an impasse and a deal cannot be made. Redstone was convinced that Huizenga was pulling his standard ploy and instructed his team to let him go. Redstone fondly remembered that Huizenga waited at the elevator for a long time before he realized no one was going to urge him to come back to the table. Some negotiators get startled in such difficult moments and make the demanded concession. They compromise because they focus on their own potential losses but fail to consider the risks and consequences of no-deal for the other side.

Dealing with Hardball Tactics

There are no golden rules for how to respond effectively to power tactics except to use your knowledge, experience, intuition, and best judgment in the moment. Here are some general tactics that might work:

Ignoring. Sometimes it is better to ignore hardball tactics and refrain from a confrontation that might further escalate the situation. President Trump made countless threats to 'tear up' the North America Free Trade Agreement (NAFTA) with Canada and Mexico. A year and a half into his administration, NAFTA is still 'alive'. Canada and Mexico ignored the threat instead of confronting it. Canada, for example, has been using its political leverage with the states that heavily benefit from NAFTA and these states put pressure on the White House to leave the agreement in place.

Responding. If, however, hardball tactics may have an impact on the negotiation process or outcomes, you may want to respond to them in a variety of ways that would neutralize them. For example, if the other side is threatening to leave the table, you can respond in kind, and also express your own willingness to leave the table. In this case you want to make it clear that if the other side 'plays' tough, you can also 'play' tough.

Discuss. As most experienced negotiators suggest, escalatory hardball tactics are not effective. Thus, a negotiator should look for ways to reverse the course of potential escalation and discuss why these hardball tactics are used. Try to understand why the other side is, for example, willing to walk away from the table. In sales negotiation, for example, it might be that a seller is asking a buyer to pay a higher price which the buyer is unable or not authorized by his superiors to pay. In this case, the seller might consider a further concession and make a deal. Or, conversely, a buyer is asking a seller to sell at a price which is below cost, and there is still room for the buyer to make a concession, pay more, and make a deal.

Chapter 4

INFLUENCE

Influence is at the heart of negotiation. It is, however, not easy to persuade others to change their attitudes, beliefs, values, or behaviors because it almost always meets resistance and the fear of losing control. Strangely, although social persuasion is an integral part of our everyday lives, most people, including negotiators, are not effective persuaders. There are several reasons for this. Firstly, human evolution did not prepare us to influence strangers because, for millions of years, we did not interact regularly with those outside our tribe. Today most of our interactions are with strangers whom we tend to perceive suspiciously. Secondly, the benefits of effective persuasion are underestimated by most people and thus they do not invest in learning and developing persuasion skills. Thirdly, most people are self-centered and, as written in the *Talmud*, the collection of Jewish religious laws that was written in the 4th century, *we do not see things the way they are. We see things the way we are.* Therefore, we tend to influence others from our subjective perspective rather than from their perspective. Effective persuaders see the reality of the situation as their counterparts do and influence them from that perspective. In this chapter, we will explore the principles and tactics of effective persuasion.

Prerequisites of Persuasion

Trust and openness. The process of persuading others is, essentially, a process of change. In this process, we ask our counterparties to change their minds and behaviors, and move forward in our direction. Given the bias that people have for preserving the status quo, we tend to resist letting go of the known and safe present reality and moving to an unknown and risky future reality, especially when dealing with strangers.

As negotiators usually focus on what is in their best interest during a negotiation, they will not be open to persuasion and consider a change from their stated position, unless the risk associated with the change is mitigated in some way. This again requires the building of trust and a good relationship between the negotiating parties. To do that, negotiators should consider two factors — time and pace. It simply takes time to build up social capital — relationships and trust — within the context of a negotiation, and the pace of building this capital can vary. Building social capital with an Asian negotiator can be a long and slow process compared to building it with a Western negotiator. Again, relationship and trust-building take place within a context that includes the background and culture of the individuals involved.

Control, letting go, and change. People dislike situations which they cannot control. Instead, they prefer situations where they feel in control of their actions, beliefs, or preferences. Having control over a situation makes people feel happier, healthier, and more satisfied.

In negotiation, however, the negotiator's sense of control is challenged because you are rarely in full control of the situation. Specifically, you might have to frequently reconsider and modify your initial ideas, interests, or preferences. Being in this state of transition — moving away from the present and considering a move to the future — is difficult because you have to let go of your initial ideas or preferences in order to gain something else of importance. Negotiation, from this perspective, is a dynamic process of *control-influence-resistance-change* between negotiators who have to let go of something and move forward to something else. As this is fundamentally a psychological process of adaptation, it is not always easy and takes time.

If the core essence of persuasion is creating change, the question we need to ask ourselves is: When do people change willingly? Firstly, when negotiators trust each other. Science tells us that when individuals socialize, the brain produces oxytocin, which is the trust hormone that helps us create social bonds. By spending time getting to know your fellow and counterparty negotiators, you will be in a much better position when it comes to persuading them. Secondly, show your counterpart that you care about their interests, well-being, and success. Then, they will be more likely to see things from your point of view and consider a change. Thirdly, show that the benefits of what they might give up now are lower than the benefits that they will gain in the future. Finally, give them choices to select from because having choices, even in less important matters, allows individuals to experience a restoration of some of the loss of control inherent in change.

Tactics of Persuasion

The interest in understanding the concept and practice of social influence is not new. In ancient Greece, more than 2,300 years ago, Aristotle, the Greek philosopher, suggested three principles of effective persuasion — ethos, pathos, and logos.

Ethos. A negotiator's *ethos* — their credibility — arises primarily from expert authority and reputation. Specifically, from a negotiator's relevant knowledge, skills, and good reputation. The benefit of having credibility is that individuals who are less knowledgeable will defer to your expert authority, especially when the outcome of making the right decision is critical. For example, people defer to physicians because they themselves do not have medical knowledge, and making the right medical decision is critical. Similarly, when it comes to the financial structure of a particular acquisition, individuals who are not experts in finance would defer to experts in financial analysis and deal structure. In a case where a company is sued for infringing on another company's intellectual property, a legal expert in patent laws with experience in litigating intellectual property will have significant expert authority and influence.

To become influential, you must be perceived as an expert authority in your field — whether that is selling cars or negotiating procurement contracts. Your credibility is known to those you have been dealing with, but not those who do not know you. Thus, your responsibility is to make your negotiating counterparts aware of your expertise, experience, education, and accomplishments before you try to influence them.

Pathos. The best persuaders influence others by establishing an emotional connection with them. Connecting to another person's heart, however, takes time. Effective negotiators make time for personal face-time in informal settings, learn about each other, and get a much better understanding of each other's interests, values, and goals. For example, Leigh Steinberg believes in the importance of personal face-time in negotiation. After telephone discussions with John Butler, the general manager of the Bills (a football team in Buffalo, New York) and the team's owner Ralph Wilson, over the contract of football player, Thomas Thurman, Steinberg decided to meet them face-to-face. He flew from California to Buffalo simply to get to know Wilson better. In the casual and relaxed atmosphere of a training camp at a sleepy college campus, Steinberg and Wilson spent a lot of time together and developed strong bonds in a way that, Steinberg said, they never would have in an office. The fact that Leigh Steinberg, a busy lawyer and negotiator, was willing to show up and stay for a while in the Bills' training camp meant a lot to Wilson, whom Steinberg grew to consider a good friend. "Often," Steinberg said, "there is no more powerful factor in a negotiation than taking the time to show up in person and invest yourself personally in developing an emotional connection."

In high-stakes international diplomatic negotiations, espionage agencies like the Israeli Mossad or the Center for the Analysis of Personality and Political Behavior at the CIA routinely develop personality profiles of persons of interest. For example, in the preparation for the Camp David peace negotiation between Israel and Egypt in 1978, the CIA briefed US President, Jimmy Carter, on the psychological profiles of both nations' leaders, Menachem Begin and Anwar el-Sadat. In a critical moment, Carter, aware of Begin's special affection for his grandchildren, gave Begin his autographed picture for his grandchildren and talked about a future of peace. Begin was deeply touched by the gesture. Later, Jimmy Carter, in his memoir, credited the CIA's personality profiles with giving him crucial insights that helped bring the Camp David Accords to a successful close.

Logos. Connecting to and influencing the *heart* is important but not enough. As Aristotle said, persuaders must also influence the *head* by using logical arguments. Roger Fisher and William Ury, leading authorities in negotiation, have suggested that negotiators should use reasoning and objective criteria when trying to persuade their counterparts. Logical arguments are more persuasive when they are presented vividly and in the form of a story that includes short anecdotes, metaphors, and analogies.

The influencing power of *logos*, however, is limited. Smokers, for example, are exposed to scientific data as well as gruesome pictures on the cigarette pack accompanied with warnings such as: *Smoking can cause a slow and painful death,* or *Smoking can damage the sperm and decrease fertility.* Still, they continue to smoke. Humans, unlike other species, are capable of rationalizing their behaviors and discount warnings of dire predictions because they see them as theoretical, not real or personal to them, but something that happens to other people. Thus, the persuasive argument should be targeted both to the head (using rationality) and to the heart (using emotions).

Social proof. Sometimes, when people do not know what to do or what is the right course of action, they simply look to see what other people are doing and then follow them. We are, fundamentally, imitators. In other words, we look for *social proof.* In the United Kingdom, for example, the tax department used to send a standard letter to those who had not paid their taxes on time, reminding them to do so. Still, a large percentage of citizens failed to pay their taxes on time. To help the tax department collect more taxes, the Behavioural Insights Team, founded by the UK government in 2010, modified the old standard letter. The revised letter stated: *Nine out of ten people with a debt like yours, in your area, pay their tax on time. You are in the minority.* As it turned out, many tax payers reacted positively to this new letter and the level of compliance increased immediately, bringing an additional revenue of £200 million in 12 months. This success prompted other governments to use the influencing 'power of the crowd'. In Poland, for example, tax revenue increased by 17%. In another case, in 2015, the city of Louisville in the USA doubled the collection of outstanding parking fees and fines when it sent drivers a letter that said: *The majority of drivers who receive a parking fine in Louisville pay it within 13 days.* In another case, a hotel, interested in environmental conservation, experimented with two messages: The first message read: *Please reuse the towels to save the environment.* The second message read: *Please save the environment, the majority of hotel guests reuse towels.* The second message was 33% more effective. Therefore, as a negotiator, tell your counterparts what other negotiators say or do in similar situations and provide evidence in order to make your statement more credible.

Incremental change. Most people prefer the status quo rather than venturing into the unknown, because we feel that we are in control when things remain the same. Thus, "the majority of men [and women]," as Francois de Callieres, a French Diplomat suggested 300 years ago, "will never enter upon a vast undertaking... Its magnitude will deter them." The process of change therefore must be a long process of incremental smaller changes, or as Francois de Callieres suggested, "if they [people] can be brought to take successfully one step after another they will find themselves at the end of the journey almost unaware." On the dark side of life, Benito Mussolini, the fascist Italian dictator, once said, "If you pluck a chicken one feather at a time, people do not notice." If people prefer and adjust better to small changes, instead of attempting one large change, negotiators must view persuasion and influence as a continuous process made of a series of incremental changes.

Commitment and consistency. In a residential community, drivers were driving too fast. To deal with the hazard, someone suggested placing a large six feet by three feet long sign on the homeowners' lawns that read: *Drive Carefully.* Most of the homeowners refused to put the signs on their lawns. Only 17% agreed. A smaller sign was then proposed that would read: *Be a safe driver.* Almost 100% of the homeowners agreed to place this sign on their lawns. Two weeks later, they were asked: *Would you put a larger sign on your* *lawn with the words 'Drive Carefully'?* The response was dramatic! 76% of the homeowners now agreed to this sign.

People tend to respond positively to small requests, and once they adjust to them, they are more likely to agree to bigger requests, because, as Professor Robert Cialdini suggests, they are *consistent* with the *commitment* to combat dangerous driving. Effective negotiators, therefore, should not ask for too much too early in the negotiation process. Instead, they should secure commitments to small changes and trust that people will be consistent with what they already said yes to. Recognizing this principle of small changes, commitment, and consistency, Shimon Peres suggested that negotiators will end up agreeing at the end of the negotiation to things that they would have never agreed to in the beginning. Therefore, a **no** statement at the beginning of the negotiation might very well turn into a **yes** statement at the end.

Reciprocity. Reciprocity is the old-fashioned exchange of favors, gifts, goods, or services. It is based on the social obligation of *giving* to those you wish to establish a connection with in the future, *receiving* from those who offer something to you, and *repaying* or reciprocating by giving back to those who have given to you in the past. Years ago, the first author Michael Benoliel, went to an arts and crafts market in Kampala, Uganda, and went into one of the stores to buy a souvenir. The tiny store was open but not attended by anyone. The attendant in the next store approached me. As it turned out, the owner of the unattended store was sick. The owner of the next store, the 'competitor', sold me the souvenir from the inventory of the store of the sick owner. It was a puzzling experience, but it made sense. The store's sick owner, who did not lose business that day, is now obligated to reciprocate a favor in the future. It is the old-fashioned social system based on mutual trust and reciprocity. If you wish to extend your influence, act first and do favors to others who will later reciprocate.

Liking, similarities, and common ground. When individuals like each other, this facilitates the connections between them and they are more likely to say yes to requests. Effective negotiators, therefore, identify similarities with their counterparts and connect with them, thereby proposing deals that are based on common interests and mutual benefits. This is what Robert Johnson did. In the late 1970s, Johnson realized that there was no television cable channel devoted to African Americans, which he thought could have a tremendous business potential. To get investments for his idea, he approached John Malone, the 'King of Cable', whom Johnson knew through cable industry meetings. "The biggest negotiation I did in business," Johnson said, "was to convince John Malone to invest half a million dollars in my idea, thereby creating Black Entertainment Television (BET)." To persuade Malone, Johnson tailored his pitch by appealing to the things he felt were important to him and Malone. "I knew Malone and what he believed in," Johnson said. "Malone, for example, believed in entrepreneurial initiatives and in individuals helping themselves and not relying on the government. And so, everything that I talked about with him was designed to hit these points. I had to convince him that I shared his value system in such a way that would make him invest in this deal."

When Malone asked Johnson how much money he needed, Johnson responded that he needed $500,000. Malone asked for 20% stake in his company in return, and that he would loan Johnson the rest. Johnson said yes, and a one-page agreement was drawn up immediately. The deal, which took less than one hour to put together, became a great success. 20 years later, BET was sold to Viacom for about $2 billion, making Johnson the nation's first African-American billionaire.

Scarcity. People are motivated to take action to secure resources — products, services, or time — that are in a limited supply, because scarcity signals greater value. There are two basic techniques that can be used to signal this information — 'limited number' and 'deadline'. Consumers will spend hours waiting in line to buy a new phone, tickets to a concert, or to be the first to enter a Walmart store on Black Friday because the supply is limited. Marketers have mastered the principle of scarcity by creating artificial shortages. Nike, for example, sells many Jordan sneakers. However, when a new one is introduced, Nike claims: *You have to get them now, this is a limited-edition sneaker.*

Similarly, the deadline technique is another artificial way to use the principle of scarcity, in this instance with time, in order to influence people to respond quickly. In negotiation, for example, offers will be limited by time. A car salesman will typically say: "The offer for this car is good for 24 hours only." Employers, for example, give the top candidate an 'exploding' offer that is limited by time. Stores that go out of business and liquidate their stock of merchandising always will include 'Liquidation: limited time of 7 days'.

Why does scarcity work? Human beings have evolved in environments of chronic scarce resources, where failing to hunt or to gather enough food was not uncommon. In such cases, the consequences were severe: sickness, starvation, and death. Even though the modern environment is no longer as dire, we still react to potential loss in the same way we did in prehistoric times.

How do you use the principle of scarcity in the context of negotiation? When there is a genuine scarcity of time. Otherwise, fabricating scarcity may diminish your credibility. When you are faced with scarcity, try to ascertain whether the shortage of the product, service, or time is real or is it fabricated. Do not accept it at face-value. Try to understand the reasons for the scarcity and negotiate. For example, when faced with a three-day deadline with a job offer, ask what are the reasons and, if you have a good reason to require more time, try to negotiate it.

Structuring benefits: present and future benefits. Given two options, getting one cookie now or two cookies later, most people would choose one cookie now. Why? The emotional brain treats immediate benefits as more valuable than future benefits because the brain's reward circuitry produces a larger pleasure signal when the rewards are immediate. Also, most of us treat the future as uncertain and thus believe that it might be risky to put off a reward that might not materialize. People tend to feel that it is better to get the reward that is offered now than wait for something better that may not happen. However, individuals whose self-control is high are able to delay gratification and receive greater future benefits instead of settling for a lower present benefit.

Let's assume that you have a successful business that is valued fairly at $1 billion. An interested buyer offers you the money as follows: $100 million in cash upon closing of the deal in 90 days and $900 million to be paid in 10 years based on the performance of the business. Would you take the offer? Probably not. When Diageo, the world's largest producer of spirits, was interested in acquiring Casaamigo, the tequila company that was founded by the actor George Clooney and his co-owners Rande Gerber and Michael Meldman, it offered them $700 million in cash and an additional $300 million based on the company's performance over a 10-year period. The owners of Casaamigo accepted this offer. As a negotiator, how you structure the rewards of a deal, both immediate and in the future, can make a significant difference.

Emphasize potential losses rather than just potential gains. Negotiators are more motivated to avoid losses than they are to obtain gains. As a result, information about potential losses attracts more attention than information about potential gains. For example, home owners in California were given a home energy audit of their home. Following the home energy audit, one group of homeowners was told "If you insulate your home, you will gain 50 cents a day." Another group was told that "If you fail to insulate your home, you will lose 50 cents a day." Although the potential gain was the same as the potential loss, more homeowners insulated their homes when presented with the second set of instructions, i.e. they might lose 50 cents each day.

As a negotiator, you can present your offer both in terms of potential gains as well as highlighting potential losses. For example, in the negotiation between Steve Jobs, the late founder of Apple Computers, and James Murdoch from HarperCollins, over e-book prices in the iTunes store, Jobs tried to persuade Murdoch to join iTunes by using the gain and loss frame: "Apple is the only other company currently capable of making a serious impact, and we have four of the six big publishers signed up already...If HarperCollins does not play ball [cooperate with Apple], it may get left behind by its major competitors [potential losses for failing to cooperate]."

Similarly, former US President Barak Obama, looking for support for the nuclear deal with Iran, said in the press conference on July 15, 2015: "With this deal, we cut off every single one of Iran's pathways to a nuclear program. This nuclear deal meets the national security interests of the United States. That's why this deal makes our country and the world safer and more secure. It's why the alternative — no limits on Iran's nuclear program, no inspections, an Iran that's closer to a nuclear weapon, the risk of a regional nuclear arms race, and a greater risk of war — all that would endanger our security." It was a classic framing of gain and potential losses designed to marshal support for the deal.

Sequencing. The interpretation of ideas can often depend on how they are presented and in what sequence, because meaning is often subjectively constructed based on each individual's personal and social experience. For example, what makes something expensive? Why is an object considered expensive? The meaning behind considering an object *expensive* is neither absolute nor universally accepted. The meaning of what is expensive is a construct, and if it can be subjectively constructed, it can just as easily be de-constructed.

Assume that two bottles of wine are displayed on a shelf in the following sequence: a bottle costing $15 is placed next to one costing $35. The $35 bottle of wine is perceived as expensive and thus only 20% of customers buy it. Imagine a different sequence of three bottles of wine in the following order: bottles costing $15, $35 and $60. Now, the $35 bottle of wine is not perceived as expensive and in this new arrangement, 63% of customers buy the $35 bottle of wine.

The same tactic is used in some supermarkets. When you shop in a supermarket, your eyes land automatically on the shelves that are at your eye-level and move downward to the lower shelves. In a supermarket that is licensed to sell wines, the most expensive wines are displayed in the two top shelves at the customers' eye-level. The wines in the mid-range prices are displayed in the middle two shelves, and the least expensive wines are displayed in the lower two shelves. This is not a random order. This vertical sequence is deliberately designed by the supermarket's manager to anchor customers on the high prices first.

The order of things often matters. Negotiators, therefore, should always ask: Does the sequence of a given issue matter? For example, in making concessions, does the sequence of the conces-sions matter? In making proposals, does the sequence of the pro-posals matter? In building coalitions, does the sequence of which party you approach first, second, and third matter?

Opt-in or opt-out. Modern advances in medical science have made organ transplantation a possibility; however, most individuals who need a transplant are not able to receive one because the number of organ donors does not match the need. In some countries, the number of potential organ donors is very low. For example, in Denmark the percentage of organ donors in the population is about 5% and in Germany is about 12%. In other countries the level of potential organ donors is very high. For example, in Poland, Hungary, France, Austria, and Singapore, it is over 98%. The ques-tion is why. In low organ-donation countries, the method is based on advanced voluntary consent: people *opt-in*. Thus, only those who have agreed to donate will become donors. In high organ-donation countries, in contrast, the method is *opt-out*. It is pre-sumed that people already consent and wish to be organ donors. And if they do not wish to be organ donors, they have to opt-out of the system. In Singapore, for example, you are automatically a potential organ donor. However, if you wish not to donate your organs, you have to ask the government to be taken out of the registry of organ donors.

The *opt-out* method is an effective method of influence that uti-lizes a structural change and does not require a psychological or social influencing campaign. Many individuals who were given a choice to *opt-in* to a pension fund but did not, found themselves with much lower savings than those who were not given that choice. Thus, many governments have legislated an *opt-out* pen-sion savings with many restrictions, including severe penalties in order to discourage opting out prematurely.

It is very common for a builder who sells apartments or houses to present to a potential buyer a thick contract, which already includes the interests of the builder. A typical potential buyer, however, does not present his or her thick contract to the builder. Instead, buyers try to *opt-out* from certain clauses or add a few changes to the default contract. Therefore, it is to your advantage to present your own contract as the default offer, if possible.

Many sellers — manufacturers and distributors — take advantage of the *opt-out* method. Instead of influencing us to buy more of their products, they make opting-out difficult. For instance, if you forget to pack your toothbrush on a trip, you will go to the nearest store to buy one. However, toothbrushes are often sold bundled together in groups of two or three. In this case, *opting-out* means you elect not to buy a toothbrush. Most likely you will give in instead and buy a bundle.

Use Your Senses

Persuasion tactics are not limited to psychosocial factors, like scarcity or social proof. Recent studies examined and discovered how senses like touch and smell, and temperature influence the experiences and decisions of human beings. Applying these findings in negotiation will not dramatically change the negotiation process or outcomes. However, they can be an additional factor in a range of other influencing tactics.

Touch. A study by Ackerman, Nocera, and Bargh in 2010 found that negotiators who were seated in soft chairs increased their initial offer by nearly 40% more than those who were seated in hard chairs. In addition, negotiators who were seated in hard chairs were perceived by those who were seated in soft chairs as strict and rigid, less emotional, and inflexible.

Smell. Pleasant smells positively influence peoples' moods and increase cooperation. One of the most liked scents is that of a freshly baked croissant with a fresh cup of coffee. Other smells, such as lavender, are also effective in improving a person's mood, and making them calmer and more relaxed. For example, customers spend more money when a lavender scent is diffused in a restaurant. In a pleasantly scented environment, people are more likely to change a dollar bill (i.e. be more cooperative) than in an unpleasant-smelling location. Real estate agents have long known this secret. They bring a plate of freshly baked cookies or spray the scent of cinnamon in a home they want to sell to make it appear more attractive to potential buyers. Negotiators also would do well to utilize the power of scent in their favor.

Temperature. In a study by Lawrence Williams and John Bargh in 2008, two groups were asked to hold either a cold drink or a cup of hot coffee for a few minutes. A few minutes later, they were asked to evaluate, based on documents, the personality of an individual. The 'hot coffee group' rated the individual's personality more favorably than the 'cold drink group'. Specifically, they thought the person was warmer, more generous, good-natured, and more caring. Therefore, even the temperature of the room, and that of the beverages served, can matter significantly in a negotiation setting.

Body Language in Persuasion

The skill of decoding body language gives negotiators an important source of information about their counterparts and a tool to influence them. Most negotiators, however, are neither able to read body language nor use it effectively. Some political leaders, in contrast, are skilled in the art of body language. Vladimir Putin, President of Russia, is extremely mindful of body language. His walk, for example, has been described as animalistic: he moves his shoulders forward and backward in an accentuated way to project animalistic power. The objective of this section is not to explore body language and its use in negotiation in detail since there are many excellent resources on this topic. Instead, we want to simply highlight the importance of this topic and encourage you to master it.

Why is understanding and using body language important? Professor Emeritus Albert Mehrabian from UCLA, one of the world's experts on the power of non-verbal communication, suggested that only 7% of human communication is influenced by words. Meanwhile, 38% of communication is influenced by a person's tone of voice, modulation, and pauses, and 55% is influenced by body movements. The extremely low impact of words makes sense from the perspective of human evolution. For millions of years, humans communicated by using voice and body movements, not languages. Using languages as a communication medium is relatively new, created only about 80,000 years ago.

Not only do humans pay more attention to voice and body movement than words, the decisions based on these stimuli are made in less than a minute. The reason for this again lies in our evolution, where in the harsh terrain of the wild, being able to make a snap decision was a critical survival skill. Thus, the human brain, based on voice and movements, is conditioned to make snap decisions. If you rely on voice and body movement as clues during negotiation, you must be extremely mindful of the signals that your voice and body send during the initial and subsequent encounters with your counterparts.

Chapter 5

BUILDING TRUST IN NEGOTIATION

Trust doesn't mean they tell you everything. It doesn't mean they don't posture.
But it means if they say, "We will do this," they will do it. It is credibility. It is integrity.

Scott Smith, former president and publisher,
The Chicago Tribune

The good negotiator will never find success on promises which he cannot redeem or on bad faith...
Honesty is the best policy; a lie always leaves a drop of poison behind.

Francois de Callieres, French Diplomat

For about four million years, humans were nomadic hunters and foragers. They lived in small bands of kinship of 50 to 75 individuals, gathered plants, and hunted animals. Threats to survival from competing bands for scarce resources were constant. Members of this small band relied on each other, developed close bonds, shared resources equally, trusted each other, and distrusted strangers. Trust prevailed within the border of the clan and ended at the border with outsiders.

The Agricultural Revolution, which began about 10,000 years ago, profoundly changed the hunter-gatherer way of life of humans.

Most settled in small agricultural villages of about 100 to 150 individuals and survived primarily by farming the land. Individuals within the village knew one another well, cooperated when necessary, and transacted through an economy of interdependence, relying on favors, obligations, and barter. Whereas, internally, the social bonds were strong, and trust was high, externally, outsiders were distrusted and viewed as posing risks to survival.

The mass migration from villages and the rise of cities in the modern era reduced the frequency of interactions with familiar and trusted family and community members, and increased significantly the frequency of interactions with less trusted strangers. This change, however, did not diminish the human tendency to be suspicious of strangers. Indeed, evolutionary psychologists suggest that competition for procreation and scarce resources conditioned humans to cooperate internally with trusted close kinship members and distrust outsiders. The last 2,000 years of imperialism and colonialism reinforced the attitude of distrust towards conquering outsiders who were interested in increasing access to resources (e.g., the Spaniards and the Portuguese in Latin America; the British in India, Hong Kong, and Africa; the Dutch in Indonesia; the French in Indo-China and North Africa; and the Italians in Ethiopia and Libya). It is, therefore, not surprising that strangers are viewed as competitors and met initially with suspicion and distrust. The challenge amid the interactions of human beings then, such as in business or diplomatic negotiations, is how to transition from a default attitude of suspicion and distrust to trust.

Trust is the foundation of good and lasting deals, and when there is not enough trust between negotiators, deals cannot be created. For more than two years, Telia, Sweden's largest telecom firm, and Telenor, Norway's largest telecom, engaged in merger talks in hopes of creating the largest telecom company in the Nordic and

Baltic regions. Lars Berg, Telia's CEO, and Tormod Hermansen, Telenor's CEO, shared a close relationship and a strong sense of mutual trust. However, when Lars Berg resigned from Telia, the Norwegians did not consider Berg's replacement, Jan-Ake Kark, as trustworthy as his predecessor, and the merger negotiations failed.

In the Northern Ireland conflict, which was mediated by former Senate Majority Leader George Mitchell, the outcome was different because Mitchell invested in building trust. When he agreed to mediate the decades-long bloody conflict in Northern Ireland, all who were involved believed that it was an impossible task destined to fail. Three years later he accomplished the impossible: he successfully brought the disputing parties together in the signing of the Good Friday Agreement. How did he do it? In the United States Senate, Senator Mitchell said, he learned that the ability to bring people together has less to do with formal authority than with a person's ability to gain trust. In Northern Ireland, he said, he worked first and foremost on gaining the trust and confidence of the parties involved.

The trusting relationship between negotiators facilitates the negotiation process and outcomes — it gets the deal done. When negotiators trust each other, they share more information, disclose their interests, develop alternatives, and creatively design mutually beneficial deal options. In addition, trusting parties do not feel the need to verify each piece of information, enabling the negotiations to move faster, reducing *transaction* costs, and increasing *efficiency*. When disputes do arise, either during the negotiations or after the deal is done, trusting parties are less inclined to escalate the conflict or attribute malicious or opportunistic motivation to the other side, and are more likely to look for ways to de-escalate the dispute. Rarely do trusting parties with long-standing constructive relationships rush to the courthouse. In this chapter, we will focus on the nature of trust, the foundations of trust, how to build trust, and how to restore violated trust.

Nature of Trust in Negotiation

Trust in negotiation is the willingness to make yourself vulnerable to another negotiator despite the uncertainty of the other negotiator's intentions and future actions. To trust a negotiator in the absence of a prior relationship involves risk — taking a chance that your counterpart will not act opportunistically and take advantage of your vulnerability.

Robert Johnson was too trusting when he founded Black Entertainment Television (BET). "I will tell you," said Johnson, "when I first started BET, I didn't have a lawyer in the company because I thought I could negotiate deals based on trust. I negotiated a deal for programming production and the production company drafted the agreement. I signed the deal. Well, the deal turned bad." It turned out that the agreement stipulated that Johnson had to use the production company to produce all his programming, which was contrary to what Johnson had in mind. Needless to say, Johnson was unhappy! Years later, when the owner of the production company got sick with a terminal illness, he called Johnson to apologize for not playing fair and not doing the right thing. Since this incident, Johnson is much more careful. He is aware of the risks and does not trust blindly, but rather trusts and verifies. When he sold BET to Viacom, he had a lawyer next to him throughout the deal.

Propensity to Trust or Not to Trust

The process of building trust is usually slow and long. However, in some cases it is not feasible. Why do some negotiators have a propensity to trust and others do not? John Bowlby, a psychoanalyst, suggested that an individual's capacity to trust depends on their early life experiences with their caregivers. Specifically, the extent to which the caregivers were responsive to the needs of individuals in their early life will determine their propensity to trust.

Individuals who were consistently well cared for by their caregivers experienced them as reliable and dependable because they were always available when needed. Being able to rely on caregivers gave them the confidence to explore their immediate surroundings and interact with strangers, and over time they learned to trust themselves and others. Later in life they developed an interdependent mode of operation — trusting themselves and others — and became capable of psychological attachment to others.

Individuals who were inconsistently cared for by caregivers, however, experienced them as partially reliable. Fearing that their caregivers may not be available when needed made them fearful of exploring their immediate surroundings and hesitant to interact with strangers. Seeking consistent safety, they developed a dependency mode of clinging to their caregivers, not confident enough to trust themselves and others. Psychological attachment to others and building trusting relationships with strangers is therefore challenging for such individuals.

Individuals who were consistently neglected by caregivers experienced them as completely unreliable because they consistently did not respond to their needs. Such individuals who were forced to rely entirely on themselves would develop a *counter-dependent* mode — severely distrusting others. Later in life, they developed a severe attachment disorder — unable to connect emotionally to others. In an orphanage in Europe, the children were labeled as the *children who do not cry* because they learned that their cries — calls for help — were always unanswered.

Should You Trust Your Counterpart?

As trust and risk are intimately intertwined, negotiators constantly face the disclosure dilemma. More specifically, how much information should they reveal?

Disclosure of information in legal affairs is not a matter of trust but rather a matter of law. In the United States, for example, the disputing parties in a civil procedure are entitled to discover evidence held by the parties during the pre-trial stage. The rationale of the disclosure rule is that justice rests on the discovery of full information and a level playing field. No one in this instance has an information advantage.

In business affairs, however, negotiators are not subject to the sweeping legal rule of discovery that requires the disclosure of all information. The disclosure of information in such cases is limited to what the law specifically requires. For example, do you have to disclose to your counterpart that you are negotiating, at the same time, with another party? According to American law, you are not obligated to disclose this information. However, in a particular jurisdiction in Australia, it is different. An Australian municipality started to negotiate first with Woolworth and soon thereafter, with Kohl's too, in parallel. But the municipality did not inform Woolworth as required by the Commercial Act of 1987. Woolworth sued the municipality successfully because the municipality had not complied with the law.

The question is: What are the guidelines you need to follow for disclosing information during a negotiation? First, follow the law of the land and comply when it is required. For instance, if you sell a house in the United States, you must disclose the condition of the house — the defects and malfunctions that are known to you.

Second, assess how trustworthy your counterpart is. Naturally, when trust is low, the risk of information disclosure is high. In this case, only non-critical information should be shared. Third, induce trust to expedite the trust-building process, because when the trust level between negotiators is low, they produce sub-optimal agreements that might not always be sustainable. To increase the trust level, you should take another measured risk and share more information. By moving first and 'modeling' information sharing behavior, the other side may reciprocate. If, however, your counterpart does not reciprocate, you may want to take another chance because, as Shimon Peres said, "The riskiest thing in negotiation is *not* to take a risk, so you take a risk." You hope that this time, your counterpart will reciprocate and share information with you. If, however, your counterpart still does not reciprocate, then it is evident that he or she wishes to benefit from information advantage.

To assess the risk of sharing information with a counterpart, you should consider the following trust indicators — integrity, reputation, benevolence, empathy, legitimacy, and ability — which will be described in detail in the next section. In addition, consider the consequences of a betrayal of trust, your personal risk-taking tolerance, and the broader context of the negotiation, including the cultural background of the parties involved.

Kenneth Novack had to face the trust dilemma — to trust or not trust Yossi Vardi in the negotiation to acquire Mirabilis, an Israeli company. "I had to evaluate the situation," Novack said, "taking into consideration the fact that Yossi Vardi came from Israel, a less formal business culture, one where deals were frequently made by a handshake rather than through legal documents". Novack examined the situation, recognizing that trust promotes trust, and followed his intuition, ignoring the American iron rule of putting everything in writing, and in the process, ended up making a successful deal with Vardi.

Why Negotiators Trust

Integrity. Integrity refers to the characteristics and behaviors of negotiators, specifically, to a negotiator's morality and justice, dependability, and fairness. "My general rule of thumb is not to lie," said former US Trade Representative Charlene Barshefsky, "because what kills the negotiation is when you don't believe a word the other side is saying and there is no way to compensate for that. There is no way to dig yourself back out of the hole if you are viewed as untrustworthy, unsavory, and unreliable."

In the deal between Robert Johnson, founder of BET, and Viacom, a major media conglomerate, trust, specifically the integrity of the principles of Viacom, was a key component. "I have known the two gentlemen I negotiated with, Mel Karmazin, the President and COO, and Sumner Redstone, the CEO and Chairman, for years — Sumner for 20 years and Mel for about 10. I had confidence in them," Johnson said, "I knew they would honor the deal, *not* because it was written on paper, but because they are straight shooters."

When it comes to keeping promises, "you always deliver what you say you will," said Ambassador Dennis Ross. "You never make a promise that you can't follow through on. If you say you can't do something, then it is demonstrated in facts that you cannot." Sometimes, to preserve your integrity, you must 'pay' a price. In some instances, Shimon Peres said, "I made a quick decision that may have been a wrong one but I never retreated. If you promise something and it is uneasy for you to fulfill it, don't try to say you did not promise it. When you keep your word, people will learn that your word is iron cast."

Fairness. In the early 1930s, Albert Einstein, one of the great scientists of all time, was invited to join the Center for Advanced Studies at Princeton University. In the correspondence between Einstein and Princeton, he was asked, "What is the yearly salary that you expect?" Einstein, residing in Europe at that time, replied, "US$3,000 per month." This offer was clearly very low. Princeton University, restraining its opportunistic instincts, and possibly understanding the consequences of negotiating a low offer, acted strategically. Princeton's counter-offer was significantly higher. In August 1932, Einstein joined the university where he carried out the bulk of his scientific research until his passing in 1955.

Recent research by neuroscientists has discovered that when negotiators perceive an exchange of resources (concessions) as fair, they feel good because the *amygdala*, the pleasure area in the brain, is activated. And when they perceive the exchange as unfair, they feel bad because the *insula*, the area in the brain that is associated with the feeling of disgust, is activated. Since unfair deals do not survive in the long run, Shimon Peres cautioned, "Don't try to win too much. If you try to win too much, you will lose your partner, and the art of negotiation is not to lose your partner, but to cut a deal with him or her."

Playing fair refers to two things. First, *distributive justice*. It means that the outcomes of the negotiation are perceived by the negotiators as fair — a commensurate exchange of value for value. Second, *procedural justice*. It means that the negotiation process itself is perceived by the parties as fair. The legitimacy of the courts, for example, is predicated on the belief that the legal process is equally fair to whoever comes before it regardless of race, gender, or their economic background. In contrast, in the negotiation between the Israelis and the Palestinians in July 2000, the Palestinians perceived the process as unfair because the Americans were not, as expected, impartial facilitators. The lack of trust in the process itself created a negative turning point in that negotiation. When Abo Ala, a prominent Palestinian leader reiterated the Palestinian's traditional demand that Israel, in accordance with UN resolution 242, withdraw completely from the occupied territories back to the 1967 border, President Clinton, the neutral mediator, became furious, losing all self-control. He told Abo Ala he was not negotiating in good faith and was violating an understanding Clinton had with Chairman Yasser Arafat and Prime Minister Ehud Barak. Furious, Clinton walked out and slammed the door. If Abo Ala had doubts about US impartiality before, after this interaction with Bill Clinton he was sure: the Americans were not impartial. This strong sense of unfair process was further reinforced when President Trump unilaterally declared Jerusalem the capital of Israel and promised to move the American embassy from Tel-Aviv to Jerusalem without recognizing the Palestinians' claim to East Jerusalem. Consequently, the Palestinians refused to meet with American mediators and accept their role as a neutral third party.

Reputation. When Henry Hollis sold the Palmer House in Chicago to Conrad Hilton, they shook hands on Hilton's first offer of $19,385,000. Within a week, Hollis received offers of more than a million dollars above that, but he never wavered on his word. He honored the handshake agreement.

Your reputation — good or bad — is your shadow, which always follows you to every negotiation. It will, sooner or later, be publicly known. Tactical negotiators act opportunistically by trying to get as much as possible in every deal and ignore the power of a good reputation. In the sports business, said Jeff Moorad, a successful sports agent, there is a negotiator who long ago lost his credibility in the business because of his hard ball tactics. "I don't think there is a general manager in baseball that believes him when he says that he has other teams interested [in the players he represents]."

People would come back to you to make another deal, Sumner Redstone said, only when you have a good reputation. Similarly, Robert Johnson never underestimated the value of a good reputation. He said, "It is important for me to have the currency of a good reputation. Being candid, honest, and forthright about my intentions generate future opportunities for doing business, because the more trustworthy you are, the more your counterparts are going to come to you with new deals."

Benevolence. Benevolence refers to the extent to which your counterpart cares about your welfare and your interests. Is your counterpart willing to consider your interests or is he or she opportunistic and self-interested? Effective negotiators who demonstrate a sincere concern for their counterpart's legitimate interests will be perceived as benevolent and thus trustworthy.

This was definitely not the case in the American-Mexican negotiation in 1975. Believing that Mexico had no other alternatives but to sell its natural gas to its neighbor to the north, the United States offered to buy it for a relatively low price. The American negotiators did not think that Mexico had an alternative — not to sell the gas at all. However, that is in fact, what Mexico did instead, burning off tens of millions of dollars' worth of natural gas at the wellheads instead of selling it to the US at such a low price. Following that dramatic Mexican act, the United States agreed to raise its offer substantially. Ultimately, some parties may feel that no deal with an exploitative party is better than a bad deal.

Empathy. It is not enough to understand your counterparts' points of view intellectually, 'from the head'. You should also understand their interests, needs, or aspirations 'from the heart'. Ambassador Dennis Ross believes that understanding your counterpart's feelings and conveying a genuine degree of empathy to the other side is the key to building trust. "You have your own needs," he said, "but you also have to have the capacity to put yourself in their shoes...in a way that is convincing to the other side. Then the other side can say, 'He really understands my problem, and I've got an obligation to understand his problem.'"

Empathy, as a trust-building ingredient, is important in intense and protracted conflicts, especially in crisis negotiation. Experienced crisis negotiators know that often it is less important to understand a hostage taker's substantive demands than it is to understand his psychological turmoil. Thus, crisis negotiators are trained to concentrate on connecting and managing the subject's emotional state. In recent years, the FBI's Critical Incident Response Team (CIRG) has adopted a negotiation technique designed to train FBI negotiators to 'listen' to the subject's emotions and win his or her trust. They do that by first showing respect and then expressing an understanding of the situation that comes from the heart — not criticizing, not challenging, and not intimidating.

Take, for example, the case of a recently divorced man (who had wanted to stay married) who broke into his wife's office attempting to harm her. The police were called, and after establishing contact with the hostage taker, the police crisis negotiator, who had also gone through a divorce several years before, shared his own personal difficulties. This helped establish a sympathetic common ground about marital relationships and divorce, which gradually built rapport and trust between the police contact and the hostage taker. The crisis was eventually resolved peacefully after nine hours.

Legitimacy. Perhaps the most basic ingredient of trust is the acknowledgment that the person on the other side of the table has a right to be there. It is very difficult to have a successful negotiation with someone you consider a non-entity, who has no standing or legitimacy. For three decades before the direct negotiations with the Palestinians in 1994 and in 2000, some Israeli politicians, including a former Prime Minister, claimed that there is no such thing as 'the Palestinian people' or 'a Palestinian identity'. It is therefore not surprising that the Israeli-Palestinian distrust has been so deep in the past 70 years.

One way to undermine an individual, a company, a community, or even a nation, is to continuously challenge their legitimacy to exist. During the contentious 1980s in the United States, there was a dramatic erosion in labor-management relations and trust as business executives and union leaders seemed intent on de-legitimizing each other's identity and agenda. The best-known enemy of the unions at that time was Frank Lorenzo, the CEO of Texas Air, who acquired Eastern Airlines. Lorenzo's business agenda was simple — increase profits by cutting costs. That meant cutting wages and eliminating union work rules, and that, in turn, meant de-legitimizing the trade unions.

When Charles Bryant, president of the Machinists Union wanted to meet with Lorenzo, Lorenzo refused. Bryant was told that Lorenzo "has been heard to say...that he does not 'sit down with unions'." Once Lorenzo refused to recognize the unions, the unions returned the favor, refusing to negotiate with Lorenzo, their archenemy. Challenging the legitimacy of the other side's very existence is, obviously, a frontal attack on trust.

The relationship and trust between management and labor unions in Germany is very different because they recognize the legitimate interests of labor unions and invest in building respectful and productive relationships. When I asked Dr. Sa'eb Erakat, the Palestinian chief negotiator, what advice he would give an inexperienced negotiator, he said, "Respect the other side...and don't ever undermine the concerns of the other side."

Ability. Perceived ability refers to the professional, technical, industry competence (e.g., real estate brokerage, private equity investments, or shipping), and negotiation abilities (e.g., forming coalition or thinking strategically) of a negotiator. Jared Kushner, Senior Advisor to President Trump, was completely inexperienced in diplomacy and mediating international disputes when he was appointed by his father-in-law to mediate the protracted Israeli-Palestinian conflict. He entered this role without much credibility or perceived ability. No wonder that experienced foreign diplomats tried to manipulate him.

This limited ability raises the following question: would you prefer to deal with a skilled or unskilled negotiator? Most effective negotiators would definitely prefer to deal with skilled negotiators because they know how to construct deals and behave effectively. Kenneth Novack, a highly skilled negotiator who represented America Online (AOL), and Larry Sonsini, another highly skilled negotiator who represented the counterpart Netscape, shared a high level of trust. This negotiation, said Novack, was extremely efficient because "we agreed, for example, that we wanted to be sure that there was, on both sides, a high level of confidence that the deal, once negotiated, would close. And once we established that principle, then it implied a number of things that both sides would agree to. I felt that Larry and I were able to deal with each other almost in shorthand as to what was fair and appropriate."

Repairing Violated Trust

Negotiators, intentionally or not, violate trust. When that happens, the question is: Is it possible to repair it? Contrary to the popular belief that violated trust cannot be repaired, research has shown that it can be restored, except in extreme cases.

The violation of trust is attributed to two major reasons. First, the negotiator's untrustworthy character — lack of integrity, values, or morality. Second, the negotiator's competency — their inability to perform a task. It is difficult to repair violated trust that is attributed to the person's character because the probability of repeated violation in the future is high and thus too risky. It is easier to restore trust that is attributed to a negotiator's competency because it was probably not intentional and ability can be improved. Violated trust can be repaired primarily by repentance, which includes:

- Expressing regret;
- Apologizing for committing the violation;
- Demonstrating a willingness to rectify the situation;
- Offering compensation to repair the damage; and
- Promising to change and not to repeat violations in the future.

Atonement and apology do not always work. In the negotiation between the management and the employees of American Airlines to restructure the company in 2003, Don Carty, the CEO, facilitated a sweetheart deal for the senior executives. The media discovered it and American Airlines' employees were outraged. The trust between the parties was broken beyond repair because Carty did not play fair; the employees believed that he did not care enough about their interests. His apologies were rejected, and under pressure, Carty ultimately had to step down.

Chapter 6

NEGOTIATION STYLES AND STRATEGY

The negotiation process is an unpredictable, interactive, and evolving process. You may know what your own negotiation style is but you may not always know who your counterparty will be and how they will behave at the table. Therefore, it is critically important to have a negotiation strategy that responds well to an unpredictable negotiation process. In this chapter, we identify three negotiation styles, discuss how to create value in negotiation, and present an interest-based negotiation framework.

Negotiation Styles

Distributive Negotiation. This style of negotiation is also known as *win-lose*. Distributive negotiators see negotiation as an adversarial and competitive zero-sum game, in which, like in sports, there is only one winner. Such negotiators are interested in maximizing their gains and do not care about the interests of the other side. Win-lose negotiators, therefore, do not disclose information or their interests, do not invest in building relationships and trust, exaggerate their demands, use threats and ultimatums, engage in deceptive behavior, claim more concessions than they give, and have minimal concerns for their reputation.

There are three types of distributive or claiming strategies. First is the *take-it-or-leave-it strategy*, which is essentially an ultimatum.

Most negotiators dislike and reject offers that are framed as take-it-or-leave-it even if they are superior to their best alternatives. Such offers trigger deep negative emotions that trump rational considerations. Thus, negotiators who issue take-it-or-leave-it offers risk having their offers being rejected and tainting the negotiation with negative emotions. The second strategy is using *objective standards*, such as appraisals or industry practices, because the intent is to influence the counterpart to make concessions that are based on the objective standard. The third type of distributive strategy is *anchoring,* which is based on taking advantage of information asymmetry, where one negotiator has more information than the other.

Negotiators who are not well-informed are typically trapped by the anchor. Instead of conducting due-diligence and discovering the market, they ignore market information and use the anchor to make a counteroffer. Most often, the counteroffer is not adjusted enough from the anchor. For example, as a tourist in Bangkok, Thailand, you wish to buy a product. The seller's offer is $65. Hoping to get a bargain price, you decide to be bold and offer $40. After a short negotiation you and the seller settle on a price of $45. Happily, you pay $45. Afterwards, however, you then discover that the average price of the product is $25.

One of the classic examples of distributive negotiation is the story of two sisters who quarrel over an orange. Each sister argues that she must have the orange, but does not say why they want the orange. As there is only one orange, they both argue for claiming the whole orange. After a while, they decide to compromise and split the orange, each getting one half. Later, they disclose their interests, revealing why they each wanted the orange. They discover that their compromise solution was sub-optimal because one sister needed only the juice and the other sister needed only the rind and the pulp. Unfortunately, they failed to create an integrative, win–win solution because they did not disclose their interests during the negotiation.

Integrative Negotiation. This style of negotiation is also known as *win–win* or value-creating negotiation. Integrative negotiators believe that the size of the negotiation pie is not fixed and can be expanded because negotiations are not necessarily zero-sum. Value-creating negotiators, therefore, share information, reveal their interests, search together for creative options, invest in building relationships and trust, consider the interests of both parties, and are sensitive to their reputational capital.

The classic story of mutual value-creation by Mary Parker Follett, an insightful management observer, is a simplistic and yet instructive example of creative integrative solutions:

> In the Harvard Library one day, in one of the smallest rooms, someone wanted the window open. I wanted it shut. We opened the window in the next room where no one was sitting. This was not a compromise because there was no curtailing of desire; we both got what we really wanted. For I did not want a closed room, I simply did not want the wind to blow directly at me; likewise, the other occupant did not want that particular window open, he merely wanted more air in the room.

Effective negotiators recognize the power of exchanging information and engaging deliberately in information-seeking behavior by asking questions and responding to them in order to identify their counterparties' interests and priorities. This approach is the direct way. Another way to achieve integrative outcomes is the implicit and indirect way. A negotiator may be able to indirectly speculate on what the other sides' interests and priorities are by analyzing the information that is embedded in the offers that are made, the type and size of concessions that are demanded, and the type and size of the concessions that are being made by the counterpart. Another way to achieve integrative outcomes, however ineffective, is haphazard and randomly exchanged information, offers, and concessions that satisfy both parties' interests.

Looking at negotiations from the strategic perspective of creating benefits in the long-run, the father of Paul Getty, one of the richest men in the world, suggested to his son, "You must never try to make all the money in a deal. Let the other fellow make some money too, because if you have a reputation for always making all the money, you won't have many deals."

Mixed-Motives Negotiation. Negotiation is like a symphony where harmony and discord coexist. Whereas the distributive style is competitive and the integrative style is cooperative, the mixed-motive style is a blend of both motives — cooperative and competitive — in the same negotiation. Before one can compete for value, it has to first be created. Once the money is on the table, then negotiators can compete over it.

Assume that a buyer has an opportunity to purchase a television set for $1,000 from an unknown seller. Assume also that a seller has an opportunity to sell the same television set for $700 to an unknown buyer. The buyer and the seller do not know that the other has these opportunities. If the buyer and the seller agree to negotiate with each other, there is, theoretically a positive range of $300 between the seller's and the buyer's reservation prices (alternatives).

Now assume that the buyer and the seller decide to negotiate. The three exchange offers of $650, $700, and $750, were rejected.

The fourth offer of $800 by the buyer is accepted by the seller and a deal is made. In this example, the buyer and seller are competing over the value of $300. When they settle on $800, both sides create mutual value. The seller creates an additional value of $100 ($800 less $700, the alternative deal). The buyer too creates an additional value of $200 ($1,000 less $800). Here, both buyer and seller cooperate by agreeing to negotiate over the television set, and compete over the $300. In reality, negotiations are not purely competitive or purely cooperative. They are a blend of mixed-motives.

While in this example, a negotiator uses a mixed-motive style in the same negotiation, in some team negotiations the competitive and the cooperative styles are split between the negotiators. Robert Johnson, for example, likes to separate between the two. On his team he has fighters — negotiators he calls 'attack dogs', who are unleashed to compete and claim value. He himself, however, prefers to cooperate and create value.

Dealing With Value-creators and Value-claimers

Naturally, you cannot control who your counterpart will be, or his or her negotiation style. Let's assume that your negotiation style is integrative — trying to integrate the interests of all parties and create mutual value. If your counterpart also has an integrative negotiation style, then the outcomes for both parties will be good because you will disclose your interests, trade-off between issues, make reciprocal concessions, avoid power moves like making threats and issuing ultimatums, and play fair.

However, it is possible that you will have to negotiate with a party that has a distributive negotiation style and does not care about your interests. With this kind of a negotiator you cannot create value. If you instead try to create value and continue to use an integrative negotiation style, the negotiation outcome will be poor. The outcomes for your counterparty will be good because your concessions or your disclosures of information will not be reciprocated.

When you negotiate with a distributive negotiator, you must also use a distributive negotiation in order not to lose. In this kind of negotiation, the outcomes will be average because the negotiators will not know each other's interests and will not search together for creative solutions. The implication is that negotiations are not about using a particular negotiation styles — integrative or distributive. It is ultimately about protecting your interests. Thus, you should have a repertoire of cooperative and competitive behavior and be flexible enough to use both styles when necessary. The problem is that negotiators have a preference for either the integrative or the distributive negotiation styles and cannot shift easily between the competitive value-claiming style and the cooperative value-creating style. When dealing with competitive value-claimers you can use the following tactics:

- *Call them on it.* Let the value-claimers know, tactfully and firmly, that you are aware of their tactics and explain that it interferes with productive negotiations. Furthermore, you can point out that their style is not effective and moving to a value-creating style will be more beneficial to all concerned parties.
- *Ignore them.* Sometimes, by ignoring their tactics, you may defeat them because you will not make concessions if not warranted, or disclose information if it is not reciprocal. Sooner or later the value-claimer will realize that the distributive style is not producing the expected results.
- *Respond in kind.* Having to protect your interests, you may move to value-claiming and match your counterparty's competitive

style by using hard tactics while trying to move them to a value-creating approach.

- **Leave the situation.** In independent negotiations, negotiators come voluntarily to the table to negotiate and can leave the table at any time without realizing too much cost. Sometimes, not negotiating with a value-claimer may be your best move, because you are not pressed to have a deal, especially if you have other alternatives.

Creating Mutual Value

Negotiators, when starting a negotiation, often say, "Lets create a win–win deal." The reality is that many negotiators simply do not know how to create mutual value, especially in complex deals that are associated with uncertainty — such as when managing risks or capitalizing on potential opportunities. So in that case, what are the conditions for creating mutual value and what techniques do effective negotiators use to create mutual value?

Overcoming the fixed pie bias. As long as negotiators believe that negotiations are a zero-sum game, a win–win deal is not possible. Thus, negotiators should give and take over multiple issues, which provides an opportunity to trade-off between issues and thus expand the pie.

Working together. A single negotiator, with best intentions, cannot create value alone. In a one-on-one negotiation, for example, it takes both negotiators, working creatively together, to create value.

Create the right atmosphere. Motivated and creative negotiators can create win–win deals by setting the right spirit of the negotiation by refraining from using power moves like threats and ultimatums. As negotiations are essentially between people, effective negotiators operate on two levels simultaneously: negotiating the substantive issues like price or terms of payment, and managing the psychosocial dynamics between the negotiators, such as relationships, trust, and conflicts.

Techniques for Creating Mutual Value

Bundling and logrolling. Effective negotiators do not negotiate one single issue at a time because this implies that there is a fixed pie, and it usually leads to a win-lose scenario. Instead, they bundle several issues together (e.g., price with terms of payment, price with quantity, or price with terms of payments and quantity). Trade-offs can be made only when several issues are bundled together.

How do you bundle issues together and trade-off? The principle of bundling issues involves placing an issue that is of a high value to you (for example, price) with another that you consider to be of low value (for example, warranty). When you trade-off on issues, you can then keep your high-value issue (price) and give your low-value issue (warranty) away to the other party. The other party, in return, will allow you to keep your high-value issue (price) because your low-value issue (warranty) is, in fact, of a high value to them. If your low-value issue is also considered to be a low-value issue to the other party, then they will reject the trade-off. Thus, it is important for you to know what the other party considers to be the high-value issues.

Capitalizing on differences in interests. Trade-offs can be made between negotiators when they do not place equal importance on the same issues. In a set of issues such as salary, benefits, duration of the contract, and a signing bonus, some issues are more important to you than others. For this reason, win–win negotiators are able to make trade-offs based on the difference in the interests of each party.

Capitalizing on differences in risk tolerance. Some negotiators are more comfortable with high-risk situations than others. As a win–win and risk-taking negotiator, it is possible for you to design a deal where you assume more risk and receive more benefits while your counterpart, who is also a win–win negotiator but is risk-averse, assumes a lower level of risk but receives fewer benefits from the deal.

Interest-based Negotiation

One mistake that negotiators often make is to turn the negotiation process into a contest of positions. Some are hard negotiators — they distrust others, are inflexible, and demand one-sided gains — and others are soft negotiators — they consider the other party to be a friend, make concessions easily, trust others, disclose their bottom line, yield to pressure, and insist on coming to an agreement. Instead of utilizing hard or soft negotiation styles, effective negotiators identify and negotiate over interests.

Interest-based negotiators have a clear understanding of why they want what they want, and realize that the other party has its own set of interests to achieve. Believing that both parties' interests can be achieved, the negotiation process then becomes about constructive problem-solving. The interest-based negotiation is based on a number of principles.

Focus on interests. In the example of the two sisters quarreling over an orange, they focused on their positions, on the *what* — "I need the orange" — and not on their underlying interests — *why* they need the orange. The question that they should have asked is,

"Why do you need the orange?" As it turned out, one sister only needed the rind and the pulp in order to make a cake. The other sister only needed the orange juice to drink it. From the point of view of positions, they were in conflict. From the point of view of interests however, they were not in conflict.

Effective negotiators, after identifying the issues, such as financial, legal, relational, or ethical, move to identifying their interests. For example, some financial interests could be paying off an outstanding loan or having enough cash flow to pay for monthly operational expenses. Some of the legal interests could be for example a binding contract based on the laws of New York state, or a clause stipulating that future disputes between the parties will be resolved only by arbitration and according to the American Arbitration Association. Ethical interests, for example, could be that all the future payments to the supplier must be recorded and reported transparently, and that there will be no side deals of any kind.

Self-interested analysis, however, is incomplete. Effective negotiators identify all the relevant stakeholders and identify their interests by _mapping the stakeholders' interests_. The stakeholders include both the direct parties at the table, and those who are not at the table but still influence the deal. For example, in major mergers or acquisitions, the anti-trust division of the US Department of Justice is not at the negotiation table but has the power to approve or not any pending significant merger or acquisition. Thus, the interests of the stakeholders who are not at the table must also be identified and analyzed.

Negotiating large deals extend well beyond the direct negotiators at the table and the stakeholders who are not at the table. They also include individuals or entities that do not have a direct stake in the negotiation but can influence the outcomes of a deal. They are the _influencers_. Thus, the _influencers_ should be identified and used. For example, during the Obama presidency, Israel mastered the art of influencing the White House by constantly courting members of the US Congress who in turn tried to influence the Obama administration in regard to the Middle East negotiations. It is not uncommon for politicians to exert their great influence while they are far away from the negotiation table.

Develop options for joint gains. Instead of limiting their thinking to developing only one or two options, both parties should brainstorm jointly and explore many possible options. Not only does creative thinking help both parties to move away from a zero-sum game and 'expand the pie', it also promotes a better working relationship between the parties.

Use objective criteria and standards. Negotiations are more effective when the negotiation is based on acceptable and objective criteria, such as precedents, industry standards, or recognized professional practices. This makes the agreement fair and also makes it easier to explain the rationale to one's constituents. For instance, two house sellers both quote a price for their houses. The first seller sets the price arbitrarily and based on their emotions and attachment to the house. The second seller provides the potential buyer with a certified appraisal from a registered appraisal company. The second seller's quote is clearly more solid as it is based on a well-accepted practice of setting house prices.

Separate the people from the problem. Every negotiation has two basic elements: issues and people. Effective negotiators separate the people issues (e.g., emotions, relationships, or disagreements) from the substantive issues (e.g., price or delivery date). It is, therefore, unwise to link issues to people and make concessions on the issues in the hope of pleasing the other party and having a good relationship. Develop good relationships independent of the issues.

Best alternative to a negotiated agreement (BATNA). As negotiations are unpredictable, effective negotiators always ask themselves: If there is no deal, what is my best option? A BATNA is the best option that you will exercise if there is no deal.

A BATNA may be attractive or not, but you always have one. Let's assume that you have a job offer of $5,000 a month from employer A. To improve your salary, you negotiate with employer B who offers you a monthly salary of $4,400 a month. Assuming that all other factors are the same, your BATNA to employer B is the offer from employer A because it is more attractive and therefore superior.

There are, however, situations where the BATNA is unattractive. Assume that a particular company is performing poorly and the owner wishes to sell it. Unfortunately, they discover that no one is interested in buying this company. The company still has a BATNA, however, in this case it is not attractive. The alternative to selling the company to one interested buyer would be to liquidate by selling its assets cheaply.

Exchange information before making a decision. Sometimes negotiators come to the table with a pre-determined set of solutions, and try to impose the solution on the other party. Negotiators need to realize that before making decisions, they should exchange information with the other party in order to jointly explore possible solutions. Solutions should come at the end of the negotiation process, not at the beginning.

Try to see things from the other party's perspective. Naturally, we see the world the way we are and not the way it is. Negotiators must make an attempt to stand in the other party's shoes and understand the situation from their perspective.

Chapter 7

WHY NEGOTIATORS MAKE POOR DECISIONS

On March 20, 2011, Deutsche Telekom AG accepted a $39 billion stock and cash purchase offer from AT&T for T-Mobile USA, Inc. The acquisition agreement included a reverse termination fee clause. It meant that if AT&T failed to close the deal, it would pay T-Mobile $4 billion in compensation, which was 10.25% of the total value of the deal, while the industry standard is only 4 to 5%. AT&T failed to anticipate the formidable resistance by regulators to the proposed acquisition, pulled out of the agreement, and was forced to pay the hefty termination fee.

Similarly, in 1993, Robert Allen, the CEO of AT&T at that time, authorized an overly generous premium to acquire NCR Corporation, a consulting and technology company. AT&T, already in the computer business, was not performing well. Instead of reconsidering its computer strategy and cutting its losses, it increased its bet on computing. The strategy failed, Allen was pushed out, and NCR was sold to SBC.

AT&T in these cases is not an outlier. What are the factors that lead deal makers to make poor decisions? In this chapter, we describe the psychological factors that negotiators often fall prey to and suggest how to avoid decision biases.

Information Availability Bias

Negotiators, in general, make decisions based on information from two sources — primary and secondary. Secondary sources of information, such as annual reports, are usually in the public domain and easy to acquire. In contrast, primary information, such as the compensation system of a given company, is privately held and difficult to get. Negotiators therefore: (1) tend to collect more information from secondary sources because they are easily available; (2) retrieve information that is easy to recall because it is presented vividly and in an attention-getting manner; and (3) end up making poor decisions that are based on partial information.

John Connaughton, the former managing director with Bain Capital, observed that managers often made decisions by relying on easily accessible information, such as industry studies. "At Bain Capital," he said, "we throw out the easily available information, and instead, rely on primary sources of information by building our point of view from the *bottom-up*." 'From the bottom-up' means collecting information on-the-ground from primary and relevant sources of information (e.g., directly from suppliers or directly from customers). Similarly, Cinven, a leading European private equity firm, prior to acquiring Odeon Cinemas, a United Kingdom-headquartered theatre chain, collected information from the bottom-up. It sent its own analysts to the field to 'hang out at the movies' and collect information on each theater site. It was not just a macro-level analysis of Odeon Cinemas in the data room. Confident with the information, Cinven negotiated a good deal: 45 million pounds less than the company's value estimated by market analysts.

Sumner Redstone, who was an investor in Viacom, did not simply assume that primary information was not available. When Terrance A. Elkes, the CEO of Viacom, and his group wanted to takeover Viacom to turn it into a private company, Redstone was outraged. He believed that Elkes was trying to 'steal' the company by buying it too cheaply. Redstone, who was just an investor holding shares of Viacom, was aware that Elkes, an insider, had an information advantage. To close the information gap, Redstone acted as a detective and met with Viacom's insiders. First, he met with Bob Pittman, who had helped to create MTV, a business unit of Viacom, and picked his brain. Pittman told him that MTV had become a very unpopular place to work in the year since Viacom had bought it, morale was low, and people were leaving in droves, but the company was doing well financially. Second, through Pittman's connections, Redstone met other insiders and at a dinner with them, Redstone learned again that MTV was doing well financially.

Information collected by individuals who are well trained in data collection from multiple sources is invaluable. Nowadays, some hedge-fund companies use former CIA and Israeli's Mossad agents who are well-versed in data collection to collect information legally. Similarly, negotiators should assume that important information is available and invest the necessary resources to get it. The second author, Geetanjali Mukherjee, works for a firm where clients contract the firm to do due diligence on potential partners before investing in them. For the price of a fraction of the deal, the client company can get salient information on their potential partner that can assure them that they are dealing with a trustworthy partner or prevent them from going into business with the wrong partner. In addition, negotiators should be mindful of giving undue importance to vivid information that is easily recalled but not necessarily more important than other information that is less top-of-mind.

Overconfidence Bias

Overconfidence influences negotiators' attitudes and decisions. In a game of chance where the probability is never more than 50/50, overconfident individuals overestimate their chances of winning and believe, however falsely, that it is around 65–70%.

Studies found that overconfident CEOs, for example, are prone to making judgment errors because they believe that they have more information than they actually have, consider their own information more important than external information, and make decisions based more on subjective judgment than on objective information. Similarly, overconfident negotiators see themselves through rose-tinted glasses; they assess themselves as more competent, honest, fair, and flexible than their counterparts. This illusion of superiority, Shimon Peres, the late President of Israel suggested, lead them to underestimate their counterparts.

This was the case of the overconfident CEO of Viacom, Terrance A. Elkes. When he tried to take over Viacom, Redstone, a small investor, decided to compete with him. It was David against Goliath. Redstone was able to acquire Viacom and become its CEO. Reflecting on this competition, Redstone wrote that Elkes' critical mistake was underestimating him; Elkes did not take the time to find out who Redstone was and failed, to his detriment, to take him seriously.

Measured overconfidence is important in some instances. In sports, for example, it keeps athletes in a game of win or lose, driven and motivated to win. In negotiation, however, overconfident negotiators risk a potential to make a deal because they tend to compromise less and turn down good offers. Such overconfident negotiators need a 'reality check' by trusted persons who are grounded in reality and advocate a realistic negotiation of what is possible.

Confirmation Bias

Deal-makers who have a high need to confirm their preconceived ideas, preferences, or feelings tend to 'filter' information by excluding non-confirming information and selecting information that confirms their preconceived ideas, preferences, or feelings. They simply distort the reality in order to satisfy themselves. Despite the overwhelming evidence that the Russians meddled in the 2016 election, for over a year President Trump repeatedly called it a hoax, a story fabricated by detractors who wished to undermined him.

Confirmation bias can be costly in any negotiation, including mergers and acquisitions. When negotiators 'fall in love' with the target company for acquisition, they will compromise the due-diligence process by exaggerating the deal's benefits and minimizing the risks. Look at the case of Teva, a global generic pharmaceutical company. It was a successful serial acquirer that got too confident. In 2016, Teva acquired Actavis Generics for $40.5 billion. Teva's CEO suggested that this deal would significantly enhance the company's financial profile and create many other benefits. Contrary to his and others' expectations, investors thought otherwise and dumped the stock. The share price of Teva sunk from $55 in 2016 to $15 in September 2017 (and later to $11). Teva's market capitalization of about $16 billon is much less than its debt burden of about $30 billion. The success of past acquisitions did not help this time because past successes sometimes trigger overconfidence, which risks future success.

Benoit Bassi, the managing director of Bridgepoint Capital in Paris was different — he never fell in love with companies. He understood the power of confirmation bias to distort the reality by minimizing the risks and exaggerating the benefits of a deal. For example, after a long period of courting FruitCo, a European company, he undertook a rigorous analysis of the company over several weeks. During this process, he found many problems and decided to 'kill' the deal to acquire FruitCo.

It is naïve to think that people can free themselves completely from a self-serving confirming bias. The challenge, however, is to minimize it by not surrounding yourself with individuals who repeat what you like to hear. Instead, subject yourself and your information to external review by independent parties who are not expected to benefit from the decision. You can appoint an official 'devil's advocate' whose role is to test your assumptions and challenge your biases.

Escalation of Commitment

Why would anyone pay more than a dollar for only one dollar? Strangely, people do. In the *dollar auction game*, a one-dollar bill is auctioned and the bidders bid in five-cent increments. Like any auction, the highest bidder gets the dollar for the amount he or she bid. However, unlike in a typical auction, the second highest bidder must pay the auctioneer the last amount that he or she bid, for which he or she gets nothing in return.

In this setup, many bidders drop out as the bidding amount approaches 70 to 80 cents, leaving usually two last bidders, who fail to understand the trap in this set-up. If they continue the bidding, they raise the stakes higher — bringing the payment for the dollar to well over one dollar. If one of them quits, he or she must pay the final amount bid to the auctioneer for no return, thereby becoming the loser. Since both bidders are competitive, they keep raising the amount, committing themselves to further escalation, each hoping the other one will blink and drop out from the bidding. As a result, the one-dollar bill is often auctioned off for four to five dollars.

The escalation of commitment is not limited to auction games. It happened to Robert Campeau, a Canadian businessman who was interested in acquiring the profitable department store Bloomingdale's. On January 25, 1988, he launched a hostile takeover bid for Bloomingdale's parent company, Federated Department

Stores. Bloomingdale's competitor, Macy's, got into the act and a bidding war began. When it appeared that Macy's was winning, Campeau topped Macy's already high offer by $500 million. Campeau thereby won the bidding battle but lost the war. In 1990, he declared bankruptcy. The Wall Street Journal concluded that the bidding war was no longer about the rational price of an asset: it was about ego.

Ordinary people in their daily lives also get trapped in escalating their initial decisions. In competitive situations, they become more committed to their initial decision and thereby escalate the situation, instead of reversing their course of actions. Can you imagine that a dispute over $909 would escalate to $100,000 six years later? Well, this was the case when a tenant installed window bars in an apartment in a co-op building in New York. After the installation, the tenant asked the co-op board to reimburse the expense, but the board refused. A legal battle erupted and six years later the disputing parties spent about $100,000 in legal fees.

It is easy to know where things start but not where they will end because people, in the process of escalation and the slow rising of negative information, say to themselves, "It cannot get worse." Well, "Guess what, it always can get worse," said Leigh Steinberg.

Whether in negotiations, auctions, conflicts, or wars, negotiators, politicians, and generals are prone to escalating their initial commitment to do something. The war in Vietnam is a classic example of a series of commitments of escalations by politicians and military generals. Sadly, they remained committed to the war even after it was clear that it could not be won.

Experienced negotiators recognize the trap of commitment to escalation — the tendency to follow a failing course of action. They commit themselves to a clearly set exit point: a reservation price, benchmark, or strategy.

Framing

From the Irish Protestants' perspective, the armed conflict in Northern Ireland was an ethnic and religious issue between the Catholics and the Protestants. But from the Irish Catholics' point of view, it was a colonial issue between Ireland and England. Others argued that it was neither ethnic nor colonial: it was a class conflict between the business people; the Protestants, and the workers; the Catholics, who resented how they were treated. In another armed conflict, the war in Vietnam, from the Americans' perspective, was about halting the spread of communism in Asia. From the North Vietnamese people's perspective, this war was about liberation from colonial powers and achieving independence, which had nothing to do with communism.

A *frame* is a point of view, a perspective, that is constructed by the mind and exists in the mind based on what we experience, see, and hear. By understanding how frames — points of view — are formed, you will be able to influence them. In an interesting study, homeowners got energy audits of their homes, and were either told that: (1) if you will insulate your home you will save one dollar a day; or (2) if you will not insulate your home, you will lose one dollar a day. Many more homeowners insulated their homes when told that they would lose one dollar because people are more motivated to prevent losses. To influence negotiators to act, frame situations not just as gains but also as losses.

People, however, react differently when situations are presented as losses in certain or uncertain situations. Imagine that you are the Vice-President for Physical Safety and your organization must install a new fire-prevention system in a high-rise building. You receive a proposal that includes two fire-prevention models — A and B. The differences in price, quality, or reliability are negligible. Based on this proposal, if model A is installed and there is a fire, the lives of 200 people will be *saved*. However, if model B is installed and there is a fire, there is a one-third probability that the lives of 600 people will be saved and a two-thirds probability that no one will be saved. Which model would you select?

Although the expected value in models A and B is the same (200 will be saved and 400 will die), most people prefer model A. When two options are framed positively as *lives saved* (in terms of gains), people are risk-averse and prefer the certain option — lives saved for sure in model A and not the uncertain option, the probability option in model B.

Now, look at another scenario of two other options, model C and model D. The differences in price, quality, or reliability between the two models are negligible. If model C is installed and there is a fire, 400 people will die. And if model D is installed and there is a fire, there is a one-third probability that no one will die and a two-thirds probability that 600 people will die. Which model would you select?

Although the expected value of these two models is also the same (400 people will die and 200 will be saved), most people would prefer model D. When options are framed as *people will die* (sure losses), people are more risk-seeking and will take actions to avoid the sure losses by choosing model D, the probability or 'gamble' option, hoping that less than 400 people will die. It is therefore not surprising that gamblers who experience losses continue to put money on the table and gamble. They hope to recoup or cut their losses, instead of quitting and taking the loss.

As people are influenced by how situations are framed, either as gains or losses, you should expect that negotiators will be more risk-averse when the situation is framed as a gain and are more risk-seeking when the situation is framed as a loss. One implication is that when the negotiation is contentious and your counterpart is threatening to leave the table, you should emphasize the losses that will arise from not concluding the deal. Similarly, in an escalated conflict, a mediator should emphasize the potential losses from not resolving the conflict. However, when the negotiation is progressing well, keep stressing the potential gains to be realized from getting a deal.

Anchoring

How do negotiators make decisions when they do not have sufficient information? Under conditions of incomplete or uncertain information, negotiators estimate the value of an unknown or uncertain object, product, service, or event by using an initial standard, a benchmark, or an anchor, and 'latch' themselves to it and use it to guide their decisions.

In an interesting study, individuals were asked to indicate how many member-states are in the United Nations (UN), but before giving their responses, they were asked to spin a roulette. Individuals who spun the roulette and landed on a high number estimated a high number of member states in the UN. In contrast, individuals who spun the roulette and landed on a low number estimated a low number of UN member states. Clearly, the individuals were anchored by the roulette's numbers, low or high. Anchors are successful only when negotiators are not well-informed, and to neutralize the anchor effect, they must research the answer rather than guess it.

As anchors are sometimes extremely effective, a strategic negotiator who detects that his counterpart is not well-informed may use them knowing that an ill-informed counterpart will get trapped in it. However, be very careful of exploiting the anchor because it may have future negative implications. Effective negotiators who are well-informed simply ignore anchors because they rely, whenever possible, on valid information.

Unfortunately, many individuals make faulty decisions based on a *self-trapping anchor*. Assume that your current salary is $X and you are contemplating a move to another organization. Most individuals will set a salary reference point, such as, "If I get an offer that is 5% above my current salary, that would be great." The reference points of 5%, 6%, or 7%, which are generally set arbitrarily, are faulty self-trapping anchors because they do not take into consideration a relevant reference point. A more effective reference is, "What is the value that I will bring to this organization and how much are they paying others who are at my equal value?"

Fixed Pie Bias

A US arms control negotiator was asked if he could craft a proposal taking into consideration the interests of both the Soviet Union and the United States. He was dumbfounded. Why in the world would the United States care about the Soviet Union's interests? That kind of thinking has been known as the *incompatibility bias* where negotiators see their interests as fundamentally incompatible, a zero-sum game.

Viewing the parties' interests as incompatible, as *win-lose*, is an attitude that has been shaped by billions of years of human evolution in environments where resources were scarce, and humans were not able to create new resources. The competition for and the quest to control resources was not limited to human beings' immediate environment. Following developments in astronomy, navigation, mapping of the seas, and the technology of warfare, countries ventured to far-away places in order to control more resources. This is the story of ancient and modern empires — Greek, Roman, Byzantine, Islamic, Ottoman, and British.

The capacity of human beings to create new resources is relatively new. It started 14,000 years ago in the Agricultural Revolution where people planted seeds and grew rice, wheat, corn, and cotton, and domesticated animals that produced eggs, milk, and cheese, increasing substantially their food supply. Creating new and additional resources continued through the industrial, scientific, and information revolutions. Now cows and chickens, for example, are injected with growth hormones in order to expedite their going-to-market. Although resources today are more plentiful than in past history, the pervasive fixed-pie, zero-sum mindset is still prevalent among human beings, especially in resource-poor countries.

In some cases, the competitive fixed-pie mindset is appropriate if the negotiation is over a single issue. For example, a real estate company is selling a parcel of land, a construction company is interested in buying it, and the only issue is price. Inevitably, the negotiation will be a competitive zero-sum negotiation. However, in most cases in life, negotiations involve multiple issues such as price, financing terms, a possible partnership in developing the land, and the closing date of the deal. In this scenario, there is an opportunity for the two parties to cooperate and create a superior agreement that benefits them both.

Endowment Effect

Your home is your castle. However, for potential buyers, it is just one of many houses in the market. The *endowment effect* is the tendency to overvalue something that you own because you are emotionally attached to it (your home, car, or wine collection). From a buyer's perspective, your emotional attachment to your assets is irrelevant and can be problematic.

Marc Fleisher is one of the most successful real-estate agents in the USA. Before he takes on clients, he interviews them in order to see how realistically they value their homes. Once he realizes that their asking price is well above the market price, he refuses to take them on as clients. He knows that the selling process will be inefficient because they have inflated expectations — they suffer from the endowment effect. Thus, they will reject a good offer because they fail to recognize that the market is the price-setting mechanism. In normal market conditions, when an asset has been on the market for too long, it is probably because it is overpriced and the owner is not yet ready to align with the market prices.

How to Avoid Decision Biases

Many economists still believe that people behave rationally. Psychologists, like the Nobel Laureate Daniel Kahneman and Amos Tversky, and behavioral economists, like Nobel Laureate Robert Schiller and Dan Ariely, have demonstrated that people are susceptible to making irrational decisions due to psychological biases. How can you avoid these irrational traps?

People think in two different ways and use either a fast or slow system (see Chapter 11 for a more detailed explanation). The fast system is intuitive, effortless, automatic, and emotional. The slow system of thinking and decision-making is logical, conscious, mindful, and effortful. In negotiation, the two systems are both necessary, but for different tasks. For example, when should you make a concession or an offer? Timing issues in negotiation are better suited to an intuitive, fast system. An analysis of five complex proposals presented in sequence requires a rational, slow system. To avoid the psychological biases that lead to making irrational decisions, you should apply the slow system of thinking. Specifically:

- **Assign a devil's advocate.** Select a credible and neutral person who does not have a vested interest in the outcome of the decision and who will challenge over-optimistic assumptions, faulty logic or biased conclusions.
- **Set clear limits.** Competitive situations trigger escalation. Set a clear exit strategy and commit to it. Unlike gamblers, resist the temptation to change your limit and try to win at all costs.
- **Neutralize stressful situations.** Negotiators, under threats or deadlines, respond from the fast and instinctive system of thinking. Avoid making decisions under pressure or fatigue. When under time pressure, negotiate reasonable timelines. When under a threat or pressure to decide, take a break to diffuse the threat or pressure. When tired from a long flight or poor sleep, take some time to recover.
- **See multiple realities.** Negotiators frame situations in order to shape a specific perception and get you to act from that frame. For example, you need a training room in a hotel. You are told that there is only one room left, the hotel is running a special and you should decide by the end of the day. Should you respond to this frame of scarcity or alternatively ask: What if I do not reserve the room today? Is the training schedule flexible? Are there other venues that offer training rooms and are also running specials? These questions and others are possible when you are disconnected from the scarcity frame and see the situation from different perspectives.
- **Consult with outsiders.** Negotiators (and executives), unlike physicians, are usually reluctant to seek a second opinion and consult with outside professionals who can bring an external perspective. The opportunity to talk through your situation and subject yourself to external analysis will sharpen your thinking and may unearth blind spots.

Chapter 8

THE INFLUENCE OF CULTURE
ON NEGOTIATION

The structure of the current global economy has made national economies more interconnected and interdependent on each other. The current trend of the rapid rise of the Chinese and Indian economies will continue in the future. It is estimated that by 2025, China will be the world's largest economic power and in 20 years, the combined three Asian economies of China, India, and Japan will dominant the global economy. Such economic developments introduce a new challenge of negotiating in different cultural contexts.

The challenge for Western negotiators is to understand Asian cultural values and find effective ways for operating successfully in Asia. The same challenge is faced by Asian negotiators who are dealing with Western counterparts. In this chapter, we describe the major dimensions that differentiate the Western and Asian cultures based on differing cultural roots, and make suggestions for negotiating successful deals across the two cultures.

Asian Cultural Roots

Culture refers to the collective mind-set of a social group that influences how they think and act. The Asian mind-set was shaped by

Confucianism, Taoism, Chinese stratagems (*Art of War*), Hinduism, and experiences with Western colonialism.

Confucius, the famed Eastern philosopher, lived in China from 551 to 479 B.C. and developed the Confucian doctrine that advocates virtuous behavior such as justice and sincerity. He proposed several principles: First, the importance of *the stability of society*, which is based on unequal relationships and hierarchical order, such as leader-follower. Second is the importance of *family harmony*, which is the basis for all other social organizations. Third is the need for *virtuous behavior*, which consists of having good manners between civilized people who have a sense of dignity. Fourth is *mastery*, which advocates self-improvement — the tenacity to acquire skills and education through hard work and perseverance. Other values include using resources wisely, spending modestly, having a respect for tradition, and reciprocating favors and gifts.

Equally important to the influence of Confucianism is that of the Taoist philosophy. Taoism advocates simplicity, contentment, spontaneity, and the principle of yin and yang, which are contrasts that complement each other and together create a harmonious whole. Harmony, however, in Taoism is not permanent. When good changes to bad and fortune to misfortune, disharmony settles. Re-harmonization is an ongoing process of mutual adjustment of two opposing forces. The Taoist principle of *reversion* — good changes to bad or fortune turns to misfortune — has been important in influencing the mindset of individuals in several Asian countries.

In Taoism, the principle of *wu wei*, can be translated into *inaction*. It does not mean literally passivity, but rather 'action-less activity' that implies accepting circumstances, yielding, and not resisting. The two principles of *yin and yang* and *wu-wei*, according to Tony

Fang, a Chinese scholar, form the foundation of the strategies in *The Art of War* and the *36 Chinese stratagems*. Readers who are interested in understanding the Chinese negotiation style further would benefit from reading these two books.

The *Art of War*, written by the Chinese general and military strategist Sun Tzu 2,300 years ago, is based on the militant principle of *ji*: planning tactics and strategies that use mental wisdom instead of physical force to win a war. From this perspective, the business arena is a competitive battlefield. Some of the combative tactics described in the book are: *hide a knife in a smile*, which means to win the opponent's trust and act after his guard is down; and *kill with a borrowed knife*, which refers to making use of others' resources for your own gain. When Japan was introduced to *The Art of War* about 1,500 years ago, it was studied immediately by military generals. To this day, Chinese managers are encouraged to read and use these stratagems in order to win in competition with foreigners.

Let's now turn our attention to the Indian sub-continent. Indian culture is religiously and linguistically diverse. It is shaped largely by Hinduism (more than 5,000 years old) and Buddhism (more than 3,000 years old), which permeate most aspects of life in India. Hindus believe that humans are subject to *karma* and reincarnation, and ultimately, by performing good deeds, they may be able to end their endless cycle of re-births and achieve spiritual salvation. The sequence of rebirths and multiple lives is, therefore, an ongoing evolutionary process.

Another major influence in India traditionally has been the caste system. Individuals born into the higher caste of the Brahmins — priests, poets, and intellectuals — have been considered to be superior to those born into the lower castes of warriors, workers, and laborers. Social hierarchy in India has embedded inequality into the fabric of society, at the same time promoting the stability of the existing order. Since the caste or social strata you are born into can influence your life in almost every way, the belief in karma and re-birth can lead to a fatalistic disposition and the attitude that the future cannot be changed. This can discourage individuals from taking initiative and action to promote change in their lives and interactions. These old historical and cultural forces are, however, changing in modern India. With modernization and increasing exposure to the West, values such as personal mastery, initiative, and innovation are more prevalent.

Colonial History

The history of colonization in Asia has left a legacy that is hard to ignore. The land of Asian countries was exploited, while their people were kept impoverished and oppressed. This history has influenced the interaction between the people of Asia and foreigners, particularly those from the West. Not surprisingly, many Asians distrust foreigners who obviously seek to gain more than they give or try to capitalize in some way on this past history. Some naïve senior Western politicians who lack experience in Asia, having had a few short meetings with Asian politicians declare: "We have excellent relationships." They are clearly mistaken. It is not easy to develop relationships in the negotiation context, least of all with a counterparty from a different culture who may be inherently distrustful of negotiators from Western cultures who do not display an awareness of cultural dimensions, and question their motivations.

Cultural Dimensions

Individualism versus collectivism. In individualistic societies, like the United States, Great Britain, Canada, and Australia, people are primarily concerned about their own personal needs and interests.

Thus, in negotiations, they act independently and express their needs. In collective societies, such as China, Japan, Korea, and Singapore, in contrast, people are concerned primarily with collective goals over individual goals and encourage self-sacrifice for the good of the whole. Self-interested behavior is discouraged and is perceived as selfish. A person's duty is to conform and contribute to the common good of the group. Thus, in negotiation, Asian negotiators will be more cooperative and loyal to the team's agenda.

Power distance. In hierarchical cultures where the power distance is high, such as in China, Japan, and India, the less powerful members know and accept that power is distributed unequally. In these cultures, power and social status are based on differences of stature, age, gender, experience, and education. Thus, in negotiation, the less powerful members refrain from expressing their opinion and rarely, if ever, challenge senior authority nor take personal responsibility to make decisions.

In more egalitarian-oriented cultures the power distance is low, for instance, in Sweden, Holland, the United States, and the United Kingdom. Rank, status, gender, and seniority, although recognized, are less emphasized. Instead, knowledge, competency, and independence are valued. Thus, in negotiation, individuals from low-power distance cultures express themselves more freely and are not as hesitant to question a higher authority. The working assumption for individuals from such cultures is that good decisions arise from competence, and from the full contribution by all the group's members, regardless of status.

Uncertainty avoidance. Uncertainty implies possible risks. One of the central rules of the Chinese bureaucracy is: "He who does nothing makes no mistakes". In *high-uncertainty* (or risk) *avoidance cultures*, like Japan, Singapore, and China, individuals prefer to operate in situations that are unambiguous, clear, and defined. As risk-averse negotiators, they make decisions after a long and careful evaluation of a large amount of information. A Chinese buyer, for example, will spend an enormous amount of time collecting information on product technology and performance, making the purchase process very long. The tendency to 'play it safe' often hinders the quest for creative, bold, and risky ideas.

In contrast, in *low-uncertainty avoidance cultures*, like Israel, USA, and Canada, individuals are comfortable in fuzzy and unclear situations. Thus, in negotiation, they do not ask many questions, do not collect a lot of information, and make quick decisions. They are open to considering bold and risky ideas.

What explains the difference in attitude towards risk? For Asian negotiators, the consequences of taking a risk and possibly failing are grave. They may lose face and might lose their jobs. If the benefits of taking a risk are significantly lower than the high costs of failing, why should one take a risk?

For Western negotiators, the consequences of failing are not as grave. Individuals are encouraged to take risks because it is the only way to create something new or different. The *Talmud*, the Jewish religious text, argues that individuals should be rewarded for the process and not necessarily the outcomes of an action or event. If the process of trying and taking a risk is not rewarded, then people will always 'play it safe'. To encourage risk-taking behavior, punishments should be eliminated and rewards should be introduced. It is not surprising that most innovations come out of nations that reward risk, including a tiny nation such as Israel, known as 'the start-up nation'.

Direct versus indirect communications. China, Japan, Singapore, and South Korea, for example, are known as *high-context cultures* because their communication style is indirect, implicit, suggestive, and vague. Asian negotiators, for example, will not say 'no' outright in order to preserve the face of their counterparty. Instead, they might say 'we will think about it'. This style of communication is purposeful because this is the virtuous way to maintain harmony and civility.

In *low-context cultures*, such as the USA, Canada, and Australia, a negotiators' communication style is direct and specific. They say what they mean directly, not leaving some things unsaid and expecting the other person to read between the lines.

This significant difference in how Western and Asian negotiators communicate make it difficult for negotiators to understand each other. Western negotiators are not familiar with the internal codes and nuances of the Asian communication style. Unable to decode high-context communication, they are at a loss. Does 'yes' truly mean 'yes'? Does 'maybe' really mean 'maybe' or 'no'? For Asian negotiators on the other hand, the low-context communication style is clear. However, they may interpret this communication in a nega-tive way by perceiving it to be offensive and threatening harmony.

To fully understand all the codes and nuances of communication in a given culture, you have to be born into that culture. Thus, by defi-nition, there will always be a communication gap. To narrow this gap, consider using a cultural interpreter to ensure that what you want to convey is heard and vice versa.

Relationships. Asians put a premium on relationships and friend-ship. They invest in building social connections of friends and col-leagues, known in China as *guanxi* and *kankei* in Japan.

Asians prefer to do business with trusted individuals, who are 'known quantities'. One's good reputation without familiarity with the other party is not enough, even at high levels. When the shipping giant, the Greek Aristotle Onassis, after the customary exchange of pleasantries proposed a joint venture to the Chinese Sir YK Pao, another shipping giant, Pao was appalled. He wondered, how could a stranger make such an offer on the first day?

The importance of solid relationships, friendship, and *guanxi* should not be underestimated when negotiating in Asia because they provide assurances that reduce the risk of doing business, which the legal system in such countries often do not. To foster relationships, Asians, known as *relationship-negotiators*, have mastered the art of hospitality, flattery, real friendship, and sometimes even false friendship. In the Chinese and Japanese relationship-focused cultures, deals evolve from previously established relationships. Deals cannot be made between strangers, unless they are introduced through the *guanxi* network. Because relationships come first and deals later, Asians will take as long as it is necessary to establish such relationships.

Westerners, in contrast, are *contract-negotiators*. They unbundle the business from the personal. For Western negotiators, deals emerge first and foremost from shared interests, and relationships might develop later during the negotiation process.

For Indians, in contrast to the Chinese and the Japanese, socializing and building relationships is much less important at the outset of the negotiation. They build relationships during the negotiations and in that sense, they are first *contract-negotiators*.

While relationships facilitate building trust, transparency, flexibility, and loyalty, they also create obligations. From a Western perspective, relationships in Asia are a double-edged sword because they are used to make new demands, re-open contracts, renegotiate previously settled terms, and demand new concessions. Westerners' refusal to accommodate new demands may well be seen as unfriendly and wind up jeopardizing relationships.

Trust. Trust can be developed from the head, known as *cognitive-based trust*, or from the heart, known as *affect-based trust*. Western negotiators develop trust from the head by making cognitive decisions about the counterpart's competency, integrity, sincerity, and reliability. In this instance, socializing is not necessary in order to establish trust.

Asians tend to trust insiders who are known and distrust strangers who carry high risk. The process of trusting strangers is very long-winded as it involves developing personal relationships, openness, mutual help, mutual understanding, and the formation of emotional bonds. Thus, for them, trust emerges from the heart, never from the head. One's experience, competence, and good reputation, although important, are not sufficient because Asian negotiators use the *family model* of relationships and trust as a prototype. The implication for Western negotiators is the need to invest patiently in the natural process of building personal trust from the heart.

Fairness. In the West, economic fairness is based on equity — *proportionality*. Those who produce more will get more rewards than those who produce less. Parties that invest more resources in a venture are naturally entitled to a greater share of the venture. Equity fairness is fundamentally based on one's power — existing resources or talent— to create value. Those who have less resources and inferior talent will get less.

In Asia, fairness is based on equality and also on need. When Thailand wanted to sell rice to China as an economic favor, China agreed. Describing the negotiation with the Chinese, a Thai negotiator commented that in the Asian tradition, the less powerful party is not expected to be as generous as the more powerful one. Fairness, therefore, is contextual and based on needs and not power. Need is measured by the economic conditions of the company with whom you negotiate, which party has more resources, and which party is in a greater need.

Fairness based on needs implies that negotiators representing wealthy foreign corporations are expected to be generous with their local and needy partners. To not act generously is to not be a good friend, as friends always help each other. However, in order to preserve 'face', the appearance of symmetry and equality must be maintained. Fairness, from this perspective, is strategic because from the Asian perspective, nothing is permanent. Power is fluid, and a high-power party today may become a low-power party tomorrow. Thus, a high-power party giving more today may be a low-power party receiving more tomorrow.

Rule of law. The West has a long tradition of a strong legal system. Contracts are solid and strictly enforced if they are violated. Among Asian nations, there are significant differences in the legal system. While Singapore, for example, has a strong legal system and strict enforcement of laws, China is still far behind.

Asian deal-makers have a long tradition of doing business without contracts because business is done within the trusted *guanxi* network that operates by the principles of sincerity and 'face'. Asians often feel insulted when their counterparts specify in detail legalism, penalties, or remedies for not honoring commitments. Contracts are merely a tangible expression of something more important — the relationships being created by the parties. Contracts are not seen as fixed instruments simply because one cannot foresee all circumstances.

Westerners manage risks by using tight contracts full of clauses for eventualities in the future — 'what ifs'. In the Asian tradition, life-changing circumstances cannot be predicted nor 'contained' in a contract. Thus, contracts are inherently deficient and can never be completely fair because they cannot deal fully with the future. Signed contracts are but a representation of current conditions and thus cannot be final. And when circumstances change and the existing contract is no longer perceived as a fair deal, it should be opened and renegotiated in order to deal with the new circumstances and strike a new and fair arrangement between the parties. Asians believe that the human touch is better than a legal contract — good relationships, friendship, trust, flexibility, 'face', and mutual considerations. The personal, social, and psychological 'instruments' deal better with the future and the unknowns than legal contracts.

We suggest that Western negotiators should restrain their legal instincts nor rush too fast to court to litigate disputes. Resolving disputes through informal influence and mediation is often the most effective way when dealing with Asian counterparts.

'Saving Face'. *Face*, or human dignity, is gained when individuals behave morally and show genuine concern for the collective's interests. Face is universal, but most salient in Asian culture which puts a premium on social harmony. To preserve face, individuals are expected to restrain their aggressive instincts, avoid direct confrontation, and not mention difficulties. Consequently, problems are not dealt with openly until they can no longer be avoided. In the Western culture, difficulties are expressed openly, discussed directly, and resolved because the focus is more on resolving the issues and less on the person.

Western negotiators should be more mindful of the significance of face in interpersonal interaction with Asians. Had American political negotiators understood the power of national face (pride), they would have refrained from labeling and shaming China publicly as a thief of intellectual property, manipulator of currency, and exploiter of trade because conflicts are managed better privately.

Time orientation. Asian negotiators are comfortable with doing multiple tasks at the same time in a less structured way because they are used to handling multiple issues in parallel.

The time orientation of Westerners on the other hand, tends to be linear and sequential. Western negotiators, therefore, prefer fixed schedules, segmentation of time, promptness, performance schedules, and set deadlines. American negotiators, for example, lose their balance when their counterparts change the agenda or rearrange the sequence of issues.

Another aspect of time is its meaning. In the Western tradition of super efficiency, time is a limited resource that needs to be managed well. Countless individuals have been trained in 'time management' in the West, while not that many in the East. For Asians, time simply exists in nature, and they believe in the natural rhythm and flow of time because each event has its own unique time and flow. Time, therefore, cannot be determined arbitrarily and restricted by schedule.

In general, negotiation in Asia takes place slowly. There are several reasons for this: First, there is the belief that a negotiator cannot maximize the benefits in a quick negotiation because negotiations are difficult and require patience and resiliency. Second, concluding a deal quickly may be seen by a negotiator's superiors as 'premature' and as if the negotiator did not try hard enough to maximize gains. Third, to move forward quickly signals anxiety and weakness. Fourth, Asian negotiators avoid taking personal responsibility and constantly go back and forth to consult with their superiors. Fifth, that explains the slow pace of negotiation is the nature of the decision-making process. To maintain harmony, diffuse risks, and save face, Asian negotiators, especially the Japanese, use a consensus decision-making process.

The pace of negotiation in the West is faster than in Asia. A Western negotiator tries to be efficient, is authorized to decide within set limits, and is willing to take responsibility. The difference in the negotiation pace between Westerners and Asians makes the negotiation process unsynchronized. For example, in the phase of preliminaries of small talks and relationships building, Westerners are very brief, while for Asian negotiators this phase includes small talk, social entertainment, ceremonies, and the exchange of gifts. In the negotiation phase, Westerners spend little time asking questions and collecting information, and quickly state their positions and make offers, while Asian negotiators are just listening, asking many more questions, and collecting information only. In the final stage of closing the deal, Western negotiators are ready to sign a deal, while Asian negotiators must take the final proposal to their superiors for review and approval.

Another aspect of time is the long-term versus short-term perspective. The time perspective of Westerners is short and interested in quick results. Asians, in contrast, are strategically long-term oriented. Thus, they believe in long-term goals that are achieved through hard work, persistence, and perseverance, especially in the face of difficulties. One should not expect immediate benefits, as Saburo Matsuo believed.

Matsuo, a Japanese salesman in a major securities company, was interested in the business of one of Japan's richest men. He stood in front of his house and bowed to him for six months, six mornings a week, but he was ignored by the rich man. One morning, however, Matsuo was caught in a heavy rain without an umbrella, and the famous rich man invited him to get into his car. There they had their first conversation about the stock market. Matsuo's patience and persistence impressed the rich man who became a new client.

This historical sense of time horizon was perhaps best expressed by the former Chinese Premier, Mao Zedong. When a journalist asked Premier Mao his opinion on the French Revolution of 1789, he said that it was too early to comment on it.

Emotions. In all negotiations there is a degree of uncertainty. Negotiators, therefore, try to make sense of the ambiguous situation by looking for clues and signs that will help them to reduce this uncertainty. One possible source is the expression of emotions.

According to the Asian-Confucian teaching, a person must be perfectly calm, exercise self-control, restrain selfish urges, and refrain from expressing emotions in public because it threatens social harmony. In such societies, only children are allowed to freely express emotions in public. Not surprisingly, Asian negotiators who are not 'permitted' to give free will to their emotions may be suspicious of strong emotional displays and distrust individuals who cannot contain their emotions, especially when they display aggressive behavior.

Western negotiators, in contrast, tend to be animated and display raw emotions because the Western culture authorizes personal expression, including the display of emotions in private and in public. Failing to understand the cultural underpinning of a particular behavior, including the display of emotions, leads directly to the trap of stereotypes. Asian negotiators, for example, may interpret the public display of emotions as uncivilized and childlike. Western negotiators on the other hand, might interpret the Asians' minimal expression of emotions as unnatural and suspicious, which often triggers distrust.

Negotiating in Asia

Successful cross-border deal-making begins with understanding the deep cultural values that drive behavior. Negotiators should be culturally informed and sensitive. However, it is not enough in Asia. Those who go to Asia as *takers* may not fare well as they do not have much to offer. Those who go to Asia as *givers* to create mutually beneficial opportunities will fare well. Here are some suggestions that may facilitate successful negotiations in Asia.

Present a long-term vision. The Asian time perspective is historical. Asian negotiators appreciate perseverance and long-term commitment based on trusted relationships that are built slowly and over time. Assure your counterparts that your goals in Asia are long-term because Asians usually distrust quick deals. You should present a vision based on shared interests first, not just benefits.

Build strong relationships and trust. Business in Asia is based on personal relationships and trust from the heart. Use skilled negotiators who know how to form emotional bonds and develop trust from the heart. Emphasize first personal relationships and friendship, openness, and understanding and help. Use trusted intermediaries to introduce you and facilitate the process of building relationships and trust. They can play an important informal role behind the scenes.

Be mindful of negotiation styles. Asian negotiators are contextual and use both cooperative and competitive negotiating styles. Foreign negotiators should not be trapped in an aggressive and

value-claiming style. To promote constructive mutual value crea-
tion, proceed with the negotiation after you have established good
relationships and some degree of trust.

Wide repertoire of behaviors. To succeed in Asia, you need to have
a wide range of skills, attitudes, and behaviors. In a culture that
tests resiliency and competes fiercely for resources, you have to be
unwilling to give up easily. In a culture that promotes harmony, you
have to be a peacemaker. In a culture where time is plentiful and
urgency is a weakness, you have to be patient. In a culture that
values symbols, rituals, and tradition, you must demonstrate
respect for the cultural tradition. In a culture that emphasizes hierarchical social relationships, you have to be respectful.

De-emphasize legalism. Relationships and trust between negotiators are much more important than just legal agreements. Do not
overemphasize legalism by presenting countless contingencies and
'what ifs'. Developing good relationships with your counterparts
is a better safeguard for taking care of any unforeseen future
difficulties.

Practice patience. Because Asians distrust quick deals, expect
deliberate delays and even breaks in the negotiation. They are
designed to test your resolve. Do not restrain yourself by setting an
inflexible deadline because time urgency in Asia is interpreted as a
weakness. Even when you are under time pressure, be calm and
project the allure that time is not of the essence. A prolonged
negotiation process is normal.

Know and commit to your objectives and bottom line. Asian negotiators often play the competitors off each other and use the long
war of attrition to erode your objectives. Your commitment to your
objectives and bottom line is critically important.

Master the substance and the protocol. Asians prepare meticulously, master the substantive issues well, and engage in continuous due-diligence. The Japanese, for example, ask thousands of questions and often repeat the same questions in order to fully understand the context of the negotiation. Be prepared to answer a lot of questions. In addition, recognize that Asian negotiators take detailed notes of everything and will use them to exploit advantages. Do the same: take meticulous notes and use the record to your advantage. Always clarify the issues and record mutual understandings in great specificity, leaving minimal room for misconstruing the issues at hand.

Be prepared for on-going negotiation. Whereas in the West a done deal is completed, in Asia, deals are not always done. Therefore, leave room for giving future concessions. Do not deplete your bank of concessions.

Be humble and fair. Asians dislike foreign negotiators who are arrogant and display superiority. Be humble about what you know and what you don't know and try to create mutually beneficial and fair deals.

Chapter 9

DETECTING DECEPTION AND NEGOTIATING WITH LIARS

He who has not good memory should never take
upon him the trade of lying.
Michael Eyquem de Montaigne

If you tell the truth, you do not have
to remember anything.
Mark Twain

In the midst of a negotiation, it can be incredibly tempting to lie or misrepresent the facts. In fact, if you can successfully lie and get away with it in a negotiation, you could have a distinct advantage over the other party. Some studies suggest that roughly half of deal-makers, given the motivation and the opportunity, lie in order to gain an advantage. The irony is that most people believe that they have been lied to in these contexts. At the same time, knowing the benefits in doing so, how can you tell if your negotiation counterpart is lying to you? How good are you at detecting lies, especially in the negotiation context?

The average person is a poor lie detector because he or she cannot differentiate between truths and lies. More specifically, the chance that you will be able to successfully detect a lie is about fifty–fifty, the same as flipping a coin. It takes considerable training in detecting physiological signs, such as voice pitch, pupil dilation, and facial micro-expressions, and training in noticing linguistic clues, such as pauses between sentences or dodging questions, that may suggest deceptive behavior.

Although deceptive behavior is not rare, the evolution of human beings did not condition us to reliably detect such behavior. Humans in early times lived in familiar and trusting small kinship groups where lying was a rarity and restricted by taboos, which meant that we did not evolve to reliably spot lies. The need to detect lies has become more critical in recent times following changes in human habitation. In the last 300 years, people have been living in larger villages, cities, and megacities, and interacting more frequently with strangers who are more likely to deceive them. Evolution, therefore, simply has not had enough time to re-wire us to better detect lies.

One of the most frequently asked questions in negotiation training is: "How can you detect lies?" The answer is: Firstly, it is difficult, precisely because humans are imperfect lie detectors. Second, to lie or not to lie is a choice. Thus, the negotiator's objective is to reduce their counterpart's motivation to lie by using specific *prevention tactics*. Third, a negotiator should learn to identify physiological signs, such as specific body language movements (covering the eyes and the mouth or touching the nose); observe facial micro-expressions (dilation of the pupil) and notice changes in galvanic skin response (GSR) or changes in skin moisture. In addition, you would do well to pay close attention to linguistic patterns. For example, liars use more words than truth-tellers, are reluctant to answer questions by dodging or avoiding them altogether or by giving long and specific answers that are filled with technical jargon.

Before we describe some prevention and detection tactics, we would like to first outline some of the different types of lies you could face in the negotiation context.

Types of Lies

The American oath administered in a court of law is: *Do you solemnly swear to tell the truth, the whole truth, and nothing but the truth, so help you God.* This oath was cleverly constructed to cover three types of lies — lies of commission, lies of omission, and lies of influence.

To tell the truth portion of the oath means not saying anything that is not true. To say something that is not true is an outright lie or a *lie of commission*. For example, in a television interview, an American TV anchor told a story about an incident when he was with US forces in a combat zone, and that he was in the helicopter that came under fire. It turned out that while he was in that combat, he was not in the helicopter that came under fire. It was a lie of commission that cost him his job. Similarly, a negotiator who says "We have two other competing offers" is committing a lie of commission if they do not in fact have any other offers.

The whole truth portion of the oath means not excluding information. A bank robber admitted to his crime but failed to mention his two other accomplices that escaped in the getaway car. This is a *lie of omission*. A negotiator who is negotiating with you and another party at the same time but does not disclose it to you is committing a lie of omission.

And nothing but the truth portion of the oath means not saying anything more than just the truth. Giving more information is a *lie of influence* because the information is designed to snowball you or to overwhelm you with a lot of information in order to manage your perception.

Which one of the three different lies — commission, omission, and influence — is the most common? Let's say that you are interested in selling your car and you take it to your mechanic. After the inspection, your mechanic tells you that a mechanical part in the car, although still functioning, is deteriorating and will soon break down completely. You could either lie to the buyer by *omission* — not mentioning the defective mechanical part, or lie by *commission* — denying that the mechanical part is deteriorating. What would you do? Most people are more comfortable in lying by omission than by commission. That is, it is easier for most people to leave out some salient information than to actively lie about a fact. Thus, in negotiation, be aware of what negotiators do not tell you.

Prevention of Deception

Masterful preparation. The motivation and temptation to deceive might increase when negotiators realize that there is an information gap — they know more than their counterpart. To reduce the risk of an information gap, you should exhaust and study all available sources of information throughout the negotiation process, because negotiators are less likely to deceive you when they realize that you are very well-informed — that you know all the issues and remember even the finer details. When your counterpart knows, for example, that you mastered his company's quarterly report, he is less likely to tell you financial facts that are different from what is in the report. It is not surprising that some international tourists, who are unfamiliar with local markets, tell so many stories about how they were deceived by greedy local merchants. Another aspect of responsible preparation is doing research on your counterpart negotiator, including on his or her reputation. As their reputation is considered a negotiators' shadow, which follows them wherever they go, try not to believe a negotiator who tries to explain away a lie and justify it by special circumstances, because deceptive behavior is often a repeated pattern, not a random or rare occurrence. Remember what Thomas Jefferson said, "He who permits himself to tell a lie once, finds it much easier to do it a second and third time, till at length it becomes habitual."

Record keeping. Negotiators from verbal cultures, like Israel or the US, talk a lot, listen poorly, and do not keep extensive notes. In contrast, negotiators from observation cultures, like Japan or Singapore, talk less, listen more, and keep extensive notes. Your counterpart might be less motivated to lie when there is a detailed written record of the discussions. Therefore, the more you ask questions, the more you listen and the more you take notes, the easier it is to detect inconsistencies, denials, and misrepresentations by referring back to the written record.

Commitment to tell the truth. Most individuals who have sworn to an oath to tell the truth will do so. In negotiation, however, you cannot administer a truth-telling oath to your counterpart, which limits your ability to ensure that the other party tells the truth. Still, you should attempt to create a spirit of honesty and truth-telling by how you initially frame the negotiation — by offering your commitment to not misrepresent facts and asking your counterpart to reciprocate by also making a similar commitment. To initiate the norm of truthful reciprocation, you should act first and disclose truthful information that is not too strategic to your negotiation. Once the norm of reciprocity of information is established, more strategic information will be exchanged over time.

Ask many questions. Of the three different types of lies, negotiators are likely to engage in lies of omission — not sharing information if they are not asked directly to share it. Thus, ask specific questions on all the issues. For example, if you do not ask about how a deal might be financed, your counterpart may not be compelled to share the financing options with you. Once you ask, "What is your organization's financing policy and how will our deal be financed?" your counterpart is obliged to address the issue. Asking specific questions is especially important when others use overly technical language (legal, medical, or scientific) that may be designed to confuse you.

Representations and warranties. In general, most negotiations are at 'arm's length', meaning that the negotiators are not obligated to disclose information, and each negotiator is acting in his or her own best interest. It does not, however, mean that negotiators are free to lie without paying the price. In countries where the rule of law is highly developed, deals are 'protected' by the law because they are based on the representations that negotiators make and the warranties that they give during the negotiation process. Thus, misrepresentations of facts, for example, would be a legal ground for walking away from an on-going negotiation, or initiating litigation if the deal was already closed. In countries where the rule of law is not developed, deals are riskier because they are not 'protected' as much by the law and the legal system. Thus, negotiators may be more tempted to misrepresent facts. Regardless of the rule of law and the availability or the absence of a legal option, negotiators should create a cooperative spirit that is based on relationships and trust, and make a mutual commitment to disclose material information and abstain from making false statements.

Contingent clauses. You are selling a parcel of land to a developer and the value of the land depends on how it will be used in the future. If the developer will build townhouses (several homes attached together), the value of the land would be lower than if they were to build single-family homes. In the negotiation you ask the developer, "What would you build on this parcel of land?" and they say that they will build townhouses. You trust the developer and sell the land. Later, you discover that the developer built single-family homes and not townhouses. Although you can sue the developer for misrepresentation, that would be a lengthy and costly process. Instead, you could have used a contingency clause which says, "If, in the future, you build single-family homes, you will pay me an additional X amount of money." If the builder's true intention is to build townhouses, he or she should not have any problem with including a contingency clause to the contract as it represents no risk. But, if the builder refuses to include a contingency clause, that may indicate that he or she is planning to build single-family homes and not townhouses.

Develop relationships and trust. Whenever possible, develop good relationships and trust with the counterpart negotiators you deal with because people are less likely to lie to those with whom they have a positive emotional connection.

Detection of Deception: Mindset and Tactics

Be psychologically comfortable. In high-trust societies, such as in Western Europe, people believe that others are basically honest and can be trusted unless proven otherwise. The default mindset is to trust. In low-trust societies, such as in Southeast Asia, people believe that others are not always trustworthy and the default mindset is to distrust. Thus, they are psychologically more comfortable to search for possible deceptive behavior, whereas individuals from high-trust societies are not.

In negotiation, however, assuming that your counterpart, whom you do not know well, is trustworthy is too risky and could be costly. Unless you know your counterpart well, you should consider the possibility of deceptive behavior and be psychologically comfortable in looking for clues to possible deceptive behavior. Similar to police detectives, you would do well to train yourself to be comfortable in being suspicious, asking direct questions, and verifying answers simply because deceptive behavior is possible.

Cluster rule. Being able to detect deception is a learned art that must be practiced with great care. Do not rush to judgment by relying on a single verbal or physical deception clue. If a person covers his mouth while speaking, it does not mean that he or she is lying. If a person asks you to repeat the question, it does not automatically mean that he is stalling for time in order to fabricate the answer. Maybe the room is just too noisy and he cannot hear you. Your judgment, therefore, must be based on a cluster of two or more verbal and physiological indicators that might suggest deceptive behavior.

Do not focus on truthful behaviors. Truthful individuals are open, composed, natural, relaxed, and do not take much time to respond to questions. They are also usually not distracted, composed, and stable physiologically, i.e. having normal blood pressure and heart rate and not sweating. Their responses to questions are specific, direct, and spontaneous. It is, however, not too difficult for deceivers to replicate these behaviors and come across as truthful. Once your mind-set is focused on what is truthful, you may fail to see the clues of untruthful behaviors that are woven between truthful statements and behaviors. In other words, pay attention to what is not right, different, unusual, or unexpected. For example, if a person is exceedingly polite, too flattering, or clears his or her throat too often before answering questions, even though they are not sick, that might indicate deceptive behavior.

Test honesty. Your counterpart never knows fully what you know and what you do not know. Honesty, therefore, can be tested by asking questions to which you already have reliable information. For your honesty test to work, ask questions to which the counterpart has a vested interest. For example, you already know from a reliable source that a particular company offers a 90-day credit line for large orders over one million dollars. You ask your counterpart, "What is your financial credit policy for large orders?" The counterpart's answer is, "It depends. Sometimes we finance deals and other times we don't. It also depends on your credit rating. The approval process can take a long time. In most cases, we extend a 60-day credit line." Note that your counterpart gave you a very long and general answer but did not directly answer your question. That is a good indicator that they may not be trustworthy.

In another case, you already know that the salespersons in a certain company get a commission for every sale they make. You ask one of their salespersons, "How do you guys get paid here?" and they respond by saying, "We get a salary only." Again, you can tell that they are being untruthful. This is a tool often used by intelligence agencies such as the FBI as well as lawyers in courts of law. They test the honesty of the person providing information or the witness taking the stand by asking questions to which they already have conclusively verified evidence.

Time and 'buying time'. People speak slowly, at a rate of 125 to 150 words per minute, but think fast — at least 10 times faster. The further in time a person gets away from the stimulus or the question that is asked, the more time the brain needs to think about something else in order to construct the answer. A person telling the truth does not need much time to think and respond to a question. Someone who is lying however, takes more time to respond because they are thinking up an answer that is different to the truth. Pay attention to the behavior that occurs within the first five seconds after you ask your counterpart a question, and to what extent your counterpart is 'buying time' to create the answer.

Failure to answer or dodging questions. When Secretary of State Rex Tillerson was asked directly, "Did you call President Trump a moron?" he said that he would not dignify the question and blamed Washington's politics for playing political games. He could have simply responded with a yes or no answer. But, he did not. He failed to answer the question and deflected it by blaming the media. Still, the common belief is that Tillerson indeed called President Trump a moron, although he never admitted it.

In other cases, the responder will dodge a question by giving a very long, not specific, and eloquent answer that is irrelevant to the question. The responder does this in order to get the listener to forget what the question was. Many politicians in the US have mastered the art of failing to respond to and dodging questions they prefer not to answer. For example, in an improvised press conference, an American congressman was asked, "From your Twitter account, a lewd photo was sent to a female college student. Was it from you or not?" The congressman responded, "If I were giving a speech to forty-five thousand people and someone in the back threw a pie or yelled out an insult, I would not spend the next two hours of my speech responding to that pie or that insult. I would return to the things that I want to talk about to the audience that I want to talk to, and that is what I intend to do." The congressman, clearly failing to respond to the question was asked again by a journalist, "All you have to do is answer yes or no, did you, or didn't you?" The congressman never answered the simple question. As it turned out, he did send the lewd photo, was convicted, and went to prison.

In another situation, former US Vice President Dick Cheney used an indecent word. In a television interview, he was asked, "Did you use the 'X' word?" to which Cheney responded, "That is not the kind of language I usually use." The interviewer continued to press him, saying, "The reports were that you did." Cheney: "Yes, that is not the kind of language I ordinarily use." Interviewer: "What did you say?" Cheney: "I expressed my dissatisfaction for Senator Leahy." Notice that he didn't specifically deny using that word, just evaded the question.

Not responding to direct questions or responding in a general and vague way during a negotiation should raise doubts about the responder's credibility. A pattern of responses such as, "I am not sure...", "It all depends on...", "I have to think about it....", or "I do not recall..." should raise doubts. Clearly, there are some sensitive questions, which may not be answered, such as, "What is your bottom line?" However, when you detect a pattern of failing to answer or dodging even simple and straightforward questions, that should alert you to deceptive behavior.

Repeating the question. Truthful negotiators do not need to 'buy time' to think and create an answer. Negotiators repeat your question to avoid an awkward silence while buying time to think and create an answer. Another form of 'buying time' to create an answer is to ask you to clarify your question: "What exactly do you mean?" This is not to say that sometimes there aren't legitimate reasons to repeat a question if, for example, there is too much noise in the room, someone abruptly enters the conference room, or the video-conference connection is poor. It just means that repeating the question can be a delaying tactic, particularly if used in conjunction with other indicators.

Attacking and blaming. Truthful negotiators, engaged in an honest exchange of information, refrain from blaming or attacking others because they do not feel that they are under investigation. Deceptive negotiators naturally feel stressed because their credibility is on the line. By attacking you — your credibility, integrity, rationality, intentions, or professionalism — they shift the focus from them to you. They hope to raise doubt about you and your behavior. A convicted executive who was charged with conspiracy, fraud, insider trading, and making false statements tried this tactic, however, unsuccessfully. In court, he lashed out and told the jurors that he was the victim of a witch hunt.

Distancing. Liars who may feel guilty distance themselves from deceptive communications by being evasive and indirect. They tend to use fewer first-person pronouns ('I') in order to distance themselves from the lies. For example, instead of saying, "I am offering you a deal that is ten percent below market rate", they would say, "This offer is ten percent below market rate." Again, this is only one indicator. Do not rely on a single clue, but instead look for clusters and patterns.

Snowballing and specificity. The snowballing tactic is used by negotiators who wish to overwhelm you with a lot of information that is designed to make it difficult to differentiate between facts that are real and information that is intended to confuse you. When your question is simple and the answer that you get is very long and detailed, perhaps it is designed to shape your perception and to confuse you. By giving you too much specific and perhaps irrelevant information, the other side may hope to confuse you more than help you. Another form of this tactic is using a lot of technical language to hide a simple answer to a straightforward question.

Pauses or delays. During the course of a negotiation, you will be able to identify the speech patterns — fast or slow pace and short or long pauses between sentences — of your counterpart. Questions that ask you to recall events from the past, such as in which hotel you stayed in London nine years ago, naturally require pausing to recall your memory. Other questions, such as whether you currently have pending offers from other buyers, should not require long pauses and delays because you know clearly the true answer. A pause, in this case, is related to whether to answer the question or not.

Throat-clearing or swallowing. When negotiators are asked questions and they intend to answer them dishonestly, they experience anxiety, discomfort, and dryness in the mouth and the throat. Thus, clearing the throat or swallowing *prior* to responding to a question may indicate an intention to deceive.

Hiding the mouth or eyes. As lying is uncomfortable for most people, they will naturally try to hide it physically by covering the mouth or the eyes with their hands or closing the eyes.

Grooming gestures. One of the ways to dissipate anxiety in stressful situations is to groom oneself — touching the hair, adjusting the tie, touching the shirt's cuffs, which President Trump does, or playing with a necklace, which Germany's Chancellor Angela Merkel does. Again, note that grooming gestures relate to anxiety and not always to deceptive behavior.

Tidying-up. Tidying-up — moving objects around you, can also indicate deceptive behavior or, at the very least, anxiety. For example, President Donald Trump, with a record of thousands of lies according to the *Washington Post*, tends to move objects on the table — a glass of water or a pen.

Anchor-point movement. A person's anchor points are those parts of the body that anchor him. When a person stands, the feet are the anchor point, and when he sits, the anchor points are his buttocks, back, and feet. As there is a connection between a heightened level of anxiety and deception, look at how the anchor points in the body are moved to dissipate anxiety. Thus, the more your counterpart's body is visible, the more you can observe movements in anchor points. Expressing anxiety by moving parts of the body does not mean that a person is lying; it is just one of the many possible signals of deception.

Now What?

Negotiators face multiple dilemmas, such as how much information you should reveal and how much you should trust the other side. Whether or not you should negotiate with someone you know is lying. In an *independent* negotiation where parties are free to walk away from the negotiation without many consequences, you might simply decide not to negotiate with a liar. There are, however, situations where the negotiators are *interdependent* and cannot walk away easily because the consequences are too costly. For example, two partners created a joint venture and now wish to dissolve it for various reasons. They have no choice but to negotiate a resolution.

When you cannot walk away from the negotiation, you have to confront the liars and expose their lies in a civil way. For example, when an incorrect statement is made, it must be challenged immediately by facts and figures. Furthermore, re-emphasize that any agreement that might be reached will be subject to strict legal review, including all the verbal and written representations made during the negotiation process.

Chapter 10

HUMAN EVOLUTION AND NEGOTIATORS' BEHAVIOR

The integration of evolutionary thinking with social sciences has led to advances in our understanding of human psychology and behavior. Evolutionary theory explains why species vary in their features and characteristics and how all species change over time in order to better adapt to their ecology. The theory argues that only the 'fittest' organisms, namely those with the most advantageous traits and abilities will adapt, survive, and reproduce, thereby passing on their genes to the next generation. You are here right now reading this chapter because your ancestors inherited the qualities that enabled them to adapt and thrive.

Evolutionary psychology applies these same ideas to understand how our mind works. Much like the way our physical traits, such as our eyesight, length of limbs, and running ability, have been shaped by evolution for better adaption, likewise the ways in which we think and act serve important social and psychological functions. For example, humans tend to follow the crowd in what is commonly known as herd mentality or conformity, and no conscious decision is required for us to engage in the behavior. We do this because there is safety in numbers. As the instinct to follow the crowd led to greater survival chances in the ancestral environment, the genes that code for herd mentality were the ones that ended up getting passed through the generations all the way to modern humans. Not surprisingly, we find that humans universally desire to belong in social groups, and while in groups they diminish their independence, conform to the majority, and move together like a herd.

A few domains have been studied by evolutionary psychologists that provide important insights into negotiation dynamics and the behavior of negotiators. In this chapter, we explore (1) the evolutionary mismatch perspective as it applies to modern negotiators' competencies; (2) mating and mate selection and their parallels with selecting negotiation counterparts and deal-making; (3) risk aversion as an adaptation that continues to pervade our everyday dealings; and (4) how humans create value through cooperation, be it on the ancestral savanna or in modern commercial contexts.

Understanding Negotiators Through an Evolutionary Mismatch Perspective

Are you an effective negotiator? Are most people, in general, effective negotiators? We asked hundreds of students, managers, and executives these questions in our lectures and seminars. Although there are some cultural and gender differences, the overwhelmingly frequent answer was, "I do not think I am an effective negotiator".

Paradoxically, many individuals who negotiate professionally and frequently, such as salespeople, lawyers, contractors, and executives, also claim that they are not very good negotiators and tend to dislike negotiating. Undoubtedly, there are many effective negotiators who do feel comfortable in the negotiation process. However, based on our informal and anecdotal 'survey', the intriguing question is why do so many individuals describe themselves as largely ineffective negotiators? The evolutionary *mismatch perspective* gives us a possible explanation. According to the mismatch hypothesis, our brains, which have been designed by evolution to prime us for membership in small, egalitarian tribes, are actually misaligned with the mammoth corporate and civic structures of the 21st century.

Humans' psychological mechanisms evolved during a period of about two million years, during which they lived mostly as hunter-gatherers in small kin-related groups of about 50 to 150 people and rarely encountered outsiders. These tight-knit communities were characterized by well-established social norms of how things should be done. Everyone was by default a trusted member of the community and the larger tribe.

In the ancestral environment, most negotiations were internal and involved trading resources between genetically related kin within the same tribe. The easily discernible visual similarities in skin color, facial features, and mannerisms between closely related kin facilitated fast and efficient trust building. Furthermore, members of a tribe shared similar social norms and expectations, such as generosity, reciprocity, and fairness based on common moral codes guided by local religions and value systems. These norms solidified social ties and prompted smooth cooperation.

However, not all negotiations were internal. From time to time, major negotiations were held with strangers outside the kin-related group or tribe. Such negotiations were often the exclusive responsibility of one or a few individuals, such as the village chief, who acted on behalf of the entire tribe.

The ancestral environment which humans are adapted for is drastically different from the modern conditions of the 19th century, where industrialization led to people working with strangers; the

20th century of massive urbanization where people live with strangers in mega cities; and the 21st century of globalization where people must deal with culturally different strangers to an unprecedented degree. Modern negotiation issues also differ drastically from those during ancestral times, such as renting an apartment, buying property, or negotiating a new job. Furthermore, dealing with strangers is unlike dealing with trusted kin-related individuals because humans (as well as other species) evolved to instinctively distrust strangers. Humans usually approach strangers suspiciously, defensively, competitively, and sometimes antagonistically because we are unsure of their motives. This deeply ingrained instinctual disposition clearly undermines our ability to create value and negotiate mutually beneficial deals.

The implication is that most individuals were not wired by evolution to negotiate well with strangers we are not related to. The same adaptive instincts that were useful in ancestral times can instead hold us back in industrialized, urban, and globalized societies rife with strangers where negotiation begins with suspicion and distrust. Perhaps, from an evolutionary perspective, we are at the very beginning of a new process of adaptation to a completely new social reality where we must negotiate primarily with strangers, and it might take many more generations to adjust and develop constructive negotiation capabilities with strangers before we can feel comfortable.

The evolutionary mismatch perspective is, however, useful because it highlights the factors that lead to cooperative behaviors within internal kin-related groups and trusted social networks that are based on emotional connections, similarities, reciprocity, fairness, liking, and trust. With an understanding of these factors, we may then know how to harness our evolved psychology to carry out more effective negotiations.

Mating and Mate Selection

Human mating for the purpose of reproduction is among one of the most researched areas in evolutionary psychology. The dynamics of human mating offer important insights for negotiation due to the parallels between our evolved mating behavior and negotiating behavior. According to evolutionary imperatives, organisms that fail to mate and reproduce will not pass on their genes, thereby constituting an evolutionary dead end. To increase the chances of getting selected for mating, the males of many species, including humans, use different strategies aimed at impressing females as well as to compete against mating rivals. Evolution importantly operates on two levels. The first level, *natural selection*, occurs when individuals have adaptive features that allow them to survive better. The second level, *sexual selection*, refers to being chosen for mating by the opposite sex in order to procreate. As organisms that survive well but fail to reproduce will not pass on their genes and thus ultimately fail to propagate, being sexually selected is arguably more important than being naturally selected. Stated differently, in evolutionary terms, there is no point to survival if it does not result in reproduction.

As such, mating and reproduction, rather than survival, are truly the engine of evolution. The evolved instinct and desire to be sexually selected is so crucial and strong that some creatures risk their own survival for the opportunity to reproduce. For example, male praying mantises risk their lives by offering their body as food bait to entice females to mate; many do not survive the encounter.

In a world where the goal is to survive and propagate, some organisms will prevail, but most will not. Corporate entities existing in a changing and competitive ecology must also play by the same rules and are subject to similar selection pressures. Therefore, corporate longevity requires continuous self-adaptation and mating with other corporate entities. Corporate death, from this perspective, is a result of not being naturally and sexually selected, for instance by failing to evolve the traits needed to adapt to changing circumstances or by failing to merge with other companies.

For example, the American sports retailer Sports Authority Inc. was established in 1929, had 463 stores in the US, Canada, and Puerto Rico, and about 15,000 employees in its heyday. However, failure to adapt to the changing retail environment and not merging with other corporations (failure to be selected to mate) led to its bankruptcy. Following a liquidation sale, it 'died', or closed its operations in August 2016. Another doomed example in the retail industry is Sears and Roebuck, an American chain of department stores. It was founded in 1886 and at its peak had about 3,500 stores. However, failure to adapt led to a decline in stores over time to 223, and in October 2018, it filed for bankruptcy. With more than $3 billion in debt, it is now near death and its chances of survival through natural or sexual selection are low.

In contrast to Sports Authority Inc., Sears and Roebuck, and many other organizations that have perished, Cisco Systems, which was founded in 1984 by two Stanford professors who were husband and wife, became the largest company in the networking and communications devices industry in 2019. During this period, Cisco successfully mated with and acquired more than 215 companies! However, because the business environment is continuously changing, Cisco Systems' natural and sexual selection in the future is never guaranteed. Just as organisms strive to mate and propagate, corporate firms need to negotiate deals and alliances with others to ensure their own longevity. But what do entities, be they organisms or corporate firms, need to do and be aware of to ensure that they mate well and achieve reproductive success?

The Different Interests of Mates

Let's consider the hypothetical scenario proposed by the evolutionary psychologist Norman Li. In a competitive market for rental housing, landlords and tenants negotiate and agree on mutually acceptable deals and both sides are legally bound to uphold their obligations. Now, imagine what would happen if a new law stated that landlords are strictly bound to uphold five-year leases even if tenants renege on their deals by not paying their obligatory rents or break a lease at any time?

At least three consequences would be likely from this asymmetry of risk. First, there would be an increase in the demand for rental leases by potential tenants due to the lopsidedly favorable terms for tenants. Second, tenants would have less disincentive to move around and will be more inclined to try and experience more new apartments. Third, assuming that the number of landlords is fixed because they could not switch to a more favorable business, landlords would adjust to the high demand and increased risks by raising prices for new leases and becoming choosier. Credit checks and references would be investigated more thoroughly.

Like the hypothetical rental market scenario involving tenants and landlords, the level of risk associated with mating between males and females also differs due to biological asymmetries in investment in offspring. In humans, the minimum investment that women must make is approximately nine months of pregnancy followed by several years of nurturance during the child's formative and highly dependent years. In comparison, men's minimum investment is a single sperm and a single act of sexual intercourse. Any additional investment from the father during the child's formative years is beneficial but not essential for the child to survive and reach adulthood. In short, females have much more 'skin in the mating game' than males. Like the hypothetical rental market situation, the different risks and interests in mating between females and males have to be managed — risk appetites have to be adjusted and interests have to be aligned.

Looking at mating from the evolutionary perspective of reproductive interests, the interest of males is to increase their reproductive success by impregnating as many females as possible. In contrast, females' interests are different — because they cannot conceive more offspring when they are already impregnated or lactating, females cannot play such a numbers game. Increasing the number of inseminations by different sexual partners does not increase the number of offspring that females can have and may in fact jeopardize the provision and protection of a committed mate. Women are therefore interested in increasing their overall reproductive success by ensuring that their sexual partners have good genes (e.g., height and strength), material resources (e.g., wealth), and the willingness to share these resources generously in the long run.

Given this asymmetrical parental investment in offspring between the sexes, women have evolved to be more cautious and selective than men in choosing mating partners. Conversely, the males of most species evolved to be more sexually eager and competitive in order to increase their mating opportunities. Across a wide range of species, males lock horns or strut their peacock tails against one another in a competitive process that allows females to assess prospective mates and pick among the most impressive males with high mate value. Ultimately, in voluntary mating, females select the males; thus, the reproductive fates of males hinge critically on female choice.

The evolutionary differences between the interests of females and males produce key challenges for both. For females, the challenge is to correctly gauge the quality or value of prospective partners before mating. Stated differently, females must assess accurately the value of potential deal partners. For males, however, the challenge is to be selected for mating. In other words, demonstrating mate value in order to get chosen as a deal partner is the primary concern for males.

Assessing Mate Value: From the Savannah to the Boardroom

Accurately assessing the value of potential mates in the harsh ancestral environment was critical. Devoid of healthcare and welfare systems, the ancestral environment was a life of constant danger, food scarcity, and potential death. Females who mated with males, who were either incapable or unwilling to provide resources, would end up struggling to fend for themselves and their offspring. It is still important in modern times for women to accurately assess the quality of prospective partners because mating with a low value man may, in general, lead to a life of poverty or near poverty, even with the support of the welfare state.

Likewise, accurate assessments of mate value in business negotiations, such as in mergers, acquisitions, joint-ventures, and other types of dealings, are also critical. Unfortunately, far too often in modern corporate mating, executives significantly misjudge the value of potential partners. For example, in 1994, Quaker Oats overvalued Snapple and mated, or merged, with them at the purchase price of $1.7 billion. According to Wall Street experts, Quaker Oats overpaid by about $1 billion. 27 months later, Quaker Oats sold Snapple for a mere $300 million.

In another case, Newell, a maker and distributor of consumer and commercial products, overestimated the value of Rubbermaid. The price to acquire Rubbermaid was $5.8 billion. In rushing the short three-week due-diligence process imposed by Rubbermaid, Newell failed to discover that Rubbermaid had inflated its value. Rubbermaid 'perfumed' itself to smell better by stuffing distribution channels using heavy promotions and deep discounts. Not long after, Newell's former CEO and chairman said, "We paid too much." Similarly, after Hewlett-Packard acquired Autonomy, a UK-based enterprise software company and paid $10.2 billion, it had to take an $8.8 billion write-off. Meg Whitman, the CEO of Hewlett-Packard at that time, admitted that Autonomy's value was overestimated. Autonomy was "smaller and less profitable than we had thought," she said.

The cost of poor mate assessment and erroneous selection can be devastating. For example, Teva, a flagship Israeli drug maker, built its recent success on a single drug, Copaxone, which was a breakthrough in the treatment of multiple sclerosis. Unable to come to market with another star drug and faced with Copaxone's patent expiration, Teva desperately wanted to mate and acquire a suitable company. Teva initially tried to mate voluntarily with Mylan, a Dutch company, and later attempted a hostile takeover with Mylan, which is akin to a forced mating. In assessing the value of Teva as a potential partner, Mylan found it to be unfit for mating and rejected its 20% premium offer over Mylan's share price at the time. After this rejection from Mylan, Teva attempted three weeks later to mate again and acquired Actavis Generics for $40.5 billion in July 2015.

What happened to Teva after this desperate acquisition? Contrary to positive expectations, roughly 14,000 employees lost their jobs, which is about one-fourth of the company's worldwide workforce. Financially, the company lost more than $57 billion in market capitalization. At one point, Teva's debt was larger than its valuation. The management executives and board members responsible for this poor mating left Teva. These devastating consequences all stemmed from a poor managerial and financial decision resulting from a hasty selection of an appropriate 'mate', much like the devastating consequences from a bad marriage.

Why do so many deal-makers fail to correctly judge the value of their mating targets for acquisitions, joint ventures, or other types of deals? The simple answer is 'skin in the game'. In modern corporations, unlike in ancestral environments, the consequences of a poor assessment of mate value is transferred to employees, investors, or taxpayers. As long as the personal and professional upside in deal-making is potentially much greater than the potential downside, deal-makers such as negotiators, executives, or bankers will be biased towards making deals even if they are not necessarily the right deals. Therefore, effective due diligence of a target for deal making, or in evolutionary terms the assessment of a potential mate's value, should be done by independent experts who would be rewarded for recommending only value-creating deals and penalized for recommending bad deals.

Interestingly, from a cultural perspective, risks tend to be transferred to others more in individualistic cultures, which are characterized by an orientation towards personal autonomy and the self over the group, than in collectivistic cultures, which are characterized by strong social bonds, collective identity, and mutual responsibility. Asian negotiators, known to be long-term and relationship-oriented, invest enormous amounts of time in getting to know their potential mates or negotiation counterparts well in order to assess their true value. Consequently, negotiations in Asia are seldom about fast, indiscriminate, or multiple matings that result in disaster or very little value. Instead, it is more often about doing deals with the right parties with whom lasting mutual value can be created.

The Mating Dance

The rental housing analogy described earlier demonstrates the different risks, costs, and benefits of mating inherent for women and men. Therefore, mating necessitates a negotiated dance of signals and moves to assess the value of prospective mates and the degree to which interests between potential partners are aligned.

Over time, our evolutionary imprints led to universal social norms and traditions that are still prevalent today. Across cultures, males demonstrate their mate value to females in the courtship phase. They send signals of interest and puff up their value by bringing flowers, offering dinner invitations, and giving lavish gifts such as diamond rings in order to woo females. Those who have desirable traits, such as good looks, health, and status, will be perceived as valuable, and will thus be in high demand. As such, high-value individuals, regardless of gender, will have higher expectations, more mating alternatives, and greater bargaining power than low-value individuals. For instance, research on the effects of mate value by the evolutionary psychologists David Buss and Todd Shackelford found that highly attractive women usually demand a partner who is good looking, wealthy, committed, *and* potentially a good father. In other words, beautiful women know their value and, in turn, they want it all.

Mate value, expectations, and bargaining power apply not only to men and women negotiating on the mating market, but also to deal-making at any level and in any context, such as corporate deal-making. For example, Waze, an Israeli company that created a real-time social network navigation system, was courted by Google and Facebook, arguably two of the world's richest tech companies. Recognizing its own high mate value, Waze had a list of mating demands, one of which was that Waze's researchers and research center will remain in Israel. Google agreed and mated with Waze successfully after paying about $1.05 billion.

Fortunately, women and men have repeatedly found common ground where their interests align, agreed to collaborate, and successfully produced and raised children in joint long-term relationships. The fundamental reason for this is the evolution of fatherhood, where males became willing to commit to the partnership and provide resources to offspring, which in turn boosted their offspring's chances of survival. As a result, men's instinct to procreate with multiple females was reshaped and adjusted to more closely resemble that of women's interests — having resourceful, reliable, and committed mates. Otherwise, voluntary mating would not have been possible. Indeed, humans are among the very few species where males actually love, nurture, and provide resources for their mates and children, including non-biological children.

Evolutionary Risk Management

Are humans averse to risks and tend to avoid them, or are they risk-seeking and tend to pursue them? Two Israeli psychologists, Nobel Laureate Daniel Kahneman and Amos Tversky (who did not receive the prize because he passed away before the prize could be given to him), sought to answer this question. In doing so, they developed *prospect theory* to explain how people make decisions under conditions of uncertainty. According to the theory, people evaluate the importance of gains or losses by using the *status quo* or the current state as a decision reference point.

The reference point is rooted in the two million years our ancestors spent hunting, gathering, and living in extremely harsh environments of continuous scarcity. Hence, living close to subsistence levels for long periods of time was the status quo. A loss of already limited resources was almost certainly detrimental to survival, such as starvation from the loss of a few days of food. On the other hand, the gain of a few days' surplus of food would not significantly impact their quality of life, especially since food could not be preserved or stored at the time. Therefore, humans evolved to focus more on avoiding potential losses than on pursuing potential gains. Indeed, the pain of losing something is often greater than the joy of gaining something. Studies show that when people are given choices between (1) getting $1,000 for sure, or (2) a 50-50 chance of getting $2,500 or nothing, they often prefer the first choice of getting the certain $1,000 over the uncertain option of getting $2,500, even though the expected value of the second choice is greater at $1,250. We simply prefer one bird in the hand over two birds on the bush.

Are people always averse to taking risks however? Research shows that people can be risk-seeking in order to avoid or prevent losses. For instance, studies have found that when people are faced with two choices, (1) a certain loss of $1,000 or (2) a 50-50 chance of either no loss or a loss of $2,500, they tend to prefer the second choice and become risk takers! When people are about to experience highly negative outcomes with certainty, such as significant losses for sure, their motivation shifts towards protecting existing resources by trying to prevent further losses. Gambling establishments in Las Vegas and other casinos thrive on losing gamblers who continue to play in order to 'salvage' their losses and usually end up losing more.

Given how our innate motivation to protect existing resources has evolved, negotiators can influence the choices of others through the proposals they make. For example, let's say your car was damaged and your insurance company offers you the following two choices: (1) an immediate $10,000 to repair your car, or (2) contest this certain offer, go to court, wait a long time, and possibly get more, say $14,000 or $15,000. Which option would you take? You know the answer.

By contrast, when losses are certain, people respond differently. For example, in a direct marketing experiment to persuade people to use a particular credit card in Israel, people were told that there are either 'many disadvantages in using cash instead of ZionCard' (i.e. a loss frame if ZionCard is not used) or 'many advantages in using ZionCard instead of cash' (i.e. a gain frame if ZionCard is used). As prospect theory would predict, the first message framed as a loss induced consumers to use their credit cards more often.

Advertisers often use the sexual loss frame when promoting products targeted at female consumers. The typical insinuation is that women will lose opportunities to be attractive and mate if they do not purchase and use those advertised products. In fact, in the 1920s, which was a period not known for being politically correct, advertisements for mouthwash and soap unabashedly claimed that women who do not maintain good oral or skin hygiene will fail to find husbands. The booming cosmetic industry is a testament to the effectiveness of the messages that play on women's desires to be seen as physically attractive, presumably in hopes of attracting high-value mates and mating successfully.

Evolutionary Cooperation

Unlike other solitary animals such as bears and various wild felines, humans are unable to survive alone against the harsh forces of nature. Throughout much of the time that humans have existed as nomadic hunter-gatherers in small tribes, we have had to rely on others for survival. It would have been very difficult for a single individual to know how to hunt, climb tall trees to reach fruits, build shelters, treat illnesses, and defend against threats all at once. However, in cooperative communities where individuals with different competencies share and negotiate exchanges of skills and resources, the chances of survival are significantly higher. Indeed, throughout our evolutionary history, tribe living expanded the capacity of humans to survive, master the environment, and thrive better.

Cooperation in small groups precedes the existence of homo sapiens and can be found across a variety of other social species. Consider the capuchin monkey, for example. They have been routinely documented to negotiate cooperative dilemmas, such as when one monkey has a sealed box containing a few nuts and another monkey has a sharp-edged flint, which can be used to pry open the lid of the box. They are, however, separated by a transparent hard plastic wall with a hole through which items can be passed. In order for this cooperative dilemma to be solved, the monkey with the flint must entrust the tool to the other monkey and hope that, after successfully opening the lid, the spoils will be shared by both. In many such experiments, these capuchin monkeys regularly demonstrate that they are willing to risk giving the flint away to their counterparts so that they can pry open the lid and retrieve the nuts, and the monkeys with the nuts also demonstrate a willingness to give away a fair share of nuts (approximately half) to their cooperative counterparts.

Hence, social creatures have evolved with the capacity to cooperate. We often think of negotiations as highly formalized processes, but many of us carry out our day-to-day negotiations across a wide range of situations without even thinking of them as negotiations. From a very young age, preschoolers already instinctively know how to 'negotiate' with their parents or caretakers for things that they want, sometimes even demonstrating the ability to form coalitions. For instance, savvy children sometimes form coalitions with doting grandparents, much to the chagrin of their frustrated parents! Like the capuchin monkeys and other social creatures, we have also evolved with an instinct to cooperate with familiar and trusted parties. The ability to cooperate does not require complex abilities like language.

Social animals instinctively cooperate most readily with genetically related kin. For example, in sun-tailed monkey communities, kin tend to favor and help each other, but this favoritism drops significantly for relatives that are genetically more distant than half-siblings. Kin favoritism can also be seen in the alarm calling behavior of ground squirrels. When ground squirrel sentries notice a predator nearby, they make a shrill noise to alert their group. Although these calls alert others of the same species in the vicinity to existing danger, they also draw attention to the caller and expose it to increased risk of predation. The calls occur most frequently when the caller has relatives nearby. Thus, such willingness to help appears to be especially intended for those who are most related. We often and quite naturally extend a hand to family members and relatives with little need for trust-building. As part of the tendency to favor those who are genetically related to us, we also tend to help those who *appear* genetically related, such as those who look or behave like us. Lamentably, this tendency gives rise to various aspects of ethnocentrism and racism, as people tend to hold negative attitudes towards those who are perceived as different based on skin color, language, or values.

We live in a global world where cooperation is no longer limited to similar individuals in small communities. Today, prosperity requires interactions and cooperation between non-kin from different cultures, countries, and regions. In this modern context, negotiators must find ways to look past their overt differences in order to develop trust and relationships. One such way is to simply extend some help and then see if the help is reciprocated. When vampire bats return to their roosts after successful foraging trips, they sometimes regurgitate food for hungry nestmates who are, for whatever reason, unable to acquire the food themselves. Such food sharing was observed to be most often directed towards kin as well as those who had also shared food with the donor before. In Old World monkeys and apes, subordinates groom higher status individuals in exchange for their support and protection. In humans, various relationship and trust-building rituals exist to grease negotiations. These rituals can range from the elaborate, such as the lengthy months spent by business partners serenading each other with dinners, lavish gifts, and entertainment before negotiating, to the simple, where small tokens are exchanged as a basic gesture of goodwill. Psychological experiments have found that even offers of relatively inexpensive gifts, such as a can of Coca-Cola or a flower, can suffice to increase people's willingness to respond positively to requests. This implies that people are sensitive to such overtures and that the economic value of what is offered may be far less important than the act of offering itself.

Human negotiation behaviors have certainly expanded impressively over the ages in response to social, economic, and technological changes. Prior to the invention of ink and paper, negotiated outcomes were dependent primarily on the presence of witnesses and the verbal words of the parties involved. Writing tools then enabled negotiated contracts to be documented and formalized. In today's modern technological age, negotiations can take place between individuals thousands of miles apart. Regardless of the form of negotiation, whether through body gestures prior to the development of languages or verbal or written forms, the fundamental requirement is the cooperation of social animals, specifically the need to see past differences, understand each other's interests, build trust, and work together to achieve mutually beneficial outcomes.

Chapter 11

THE NEUROSCIENCE OF NEGOTIATION

The study of neuroscience, or the science of brains, minds, and nervous systems, bloomed in the 1990s due to advancements in brain-imaging technologies such as electroencephalography (EEGs) and functional magnetic resonance (fMRIs), which allowed scientists to examine the human brain in a way that wasn't possible with earlier technology. Since these advancements, it was just a matter of time before neuroscience would penetrate mainstream business fields such as management and marketing, reflecting the widespread recognition that deciphering the mind will help us to better understand key human behaviors. On the one hand, such knowledge feeds human curiosity; on the other hand, people also desire such knowledge in order to gain an edge over others. Thus, it would also just be a matter of time before negotiation experts tap into this knowledge wellspring to guide their own insights.

The Human Brain and Mind: A Primer

Despite its relatively unassuming size and weight, the brain has been described as housing an entire universe within. One popular view of the human brain was proposed in the 1960s by the physician and neuroscientist Paul MacLean, who suggested that the brain evolved in terms of three layers of brain matter. Referring to the human brain as 'triune', he segmented the brain into distinct

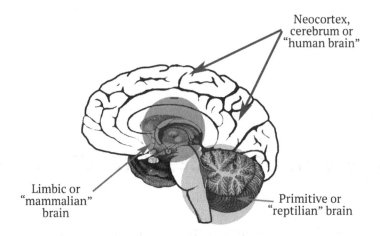

Figure 1.   MacLean's Triune Brain Model.

segments as shown in Figure 1, each reflecting different moments in the evolutionary history of how humans and their cognitive abilities emerged.

The Triune Brain Model

According to the triune brain model, the *reptilian brain* is the most primitive and sits at the base, which is also referred to as the brain stem. It includes the main structures found in the brains of reptiles and amphibians and is associated with basic vital reflexes, such as breathing and heart rate, as well as the 'fight, flight, or freeze' responses that take over when survival is at stake. The second layer of the brain, referred to as the midbrain or the *limbic system*, evolved with the emergence of mammals. Because mammals suckle their young and have strong emotional instincts for attachment, the limbic system is believed to be associated with sensory processing (i.e. sound, taste, smell, sight, and touch) and emotional reactions. As a rapid sensory appraisal system, the limbic system helps animals to interpret, within milliseconds and without requiring conscious awareness, whether something is threatening and to be avoided, or rewarding and to be approached. For instance, a stranger might walk toward you in a dark alley. Appraising the stranger as potentially dangerous will elicit defensive feelings that prime you for self-protection, whereas appraising the stranger as harmless or a potential ally may elicit a variety of feelings ranging from apathy to the desire to socially interact. This appraisal process occurs without any need for conscious awareness, although certain cues may contribute to subconscious judgment, such as whether the stranger is male, appears large, or shares similar facial features. Finally, the forebrain, also known as the *neocortex*, is the outer, and allegedly most recent layer of the human brain, and is especially developed in primates and other cognitively advanced mammals. It is associated with conscious, higher-order mental functions, such as abstract thought, planning, and the conscious appreciation of emotions, as well as complex coordination of motor and sensory functions, allowing for speech comprehension and conscious memory.

On the surface, this model of the human brain is intuitively appealing and appears consistent with the evolution of cognitive capacities from 'lower' animals to humans. For instance, the entire brains of animals such as those of reptiles and amphibians, which appear relatively early on the evolutionary scale, look like our brain stem. Thus, the reptilian brain may have served as the basis for early mammalian brains, following which early mammalian brains provided the foundations for the arrival of the human brain.

This model of the human brain also offers an easy-to-understand account of how the mind works. It suggests that all our senses, which are stimulated by the things we perceive in reality, are subconsciously analyzed by the limbic system first. Downstream activation of either the reptilian system or the neocortex depends on the limbic system's analysis, such as whether the sensory stimulus produces a sense of fear which then generates avoidance reflexes, or a sense of reward which then instigates the desire to approach the stimulus. Thus, the triune model views the limbic system as a switch that activates or suppresses either higher-order 'cortical thinking' or reptilian 'non-thinking' based on rapid, subconscious judgments of reality. This model suggests that our emotions reflect our most fundamental animalistic drives operating outside conscious awareness, which accounts for why it can be so difficult to override our instincts and biases. Furthermore, it explains why it can be difficult to be logical and highly emotional at the same time.

Imperfect Theory, Good Metaphor

Although MacLean's theory is intuitively appealing, the triune model is regarded by modern neuroscientists as overly simplistic and incorrect when scrutinized more deeply. For example, the notion that the mind becomes increasingly complex through a 'stacking' of more evolutionarily recent brains over primitive brains is largely disputed.

Despite its limitations, MacLean's theory has considerable merits. The triune brain model serves as a poetic metaphor for how the brain and mind generally works, which can be a great way to introduce neuroscience concepts to novice readers. Even if the hypothesized brain layers do not operate exactly as we would expect, they still serve as fairly accurate approximations of the associations between brain regions and mental functions. For instance, our higher-order thinking and executive functions (for example, impulse control and working memory) are indeed associated with the frontal lobes in the neocortex, and the experience of pleasure and other emotions are indeed associated with the amygdala — a brain area that underlies our reward system — in the limbic system.

MacLean's views also promoted evolutionary thinking as a way to understand the design and function of the brain, an approach which has helped to make sense of how the brain is differentially specialized across species. For example, the part of the brain dedicated to smell, known as the olfactory bulb, takes up a greater proportion of rodents' brains than humans'; this indeed accounts for the keen sense of smell that rats require for finding food and mates versus humans' relative ineptitude in smelling.

Furthermore, the idea that there are two distinct forms of cognitive processing — conscious, deliberative thinking versus nonconscious, instinctive reflexes — is supported by research in psychology. These ideas were formalized by the Nobel Laureate Daniel Kahneman in his dual process model of fast versus slow mental processes, which he referred to as System 1 and System 2 respectively.

Fast versus Slow Processing

According to Kahneman, we have two thinking systems. As illustrated in Figure 2, System 1 is responsible for our instinctive emotional reactions and gut feelings and is, thus, the reason we form first impressions or jump to conclusions, whereas System 2 allows us to critically reflect, analyze, and solve complex problems. As seemingly intelligent beings, we typically consider ourselves rational and analytical; therefore, we are under the impression that we are constantly engaged in System 2. In reality, however, we spend almost all of our daily lives engaged in System 1 and go along unquestioningly with the impressions and intuitions formed by System 1. System 1 houses automatic impulses driven by important survival reflexes and deep-seated, learned habits, which in most cases are instrumental for producing adaptive behaviors (for example, avoiding dangerous situations and making judgments and decisions quickly and effortlessly). System 2 only gets activated when we encounter something unexpected that System 1 cannot automatically process, for instance when we exert conscious effort to pay close attention to our perceptions, or when we try to understand why we feel a certain way about something.

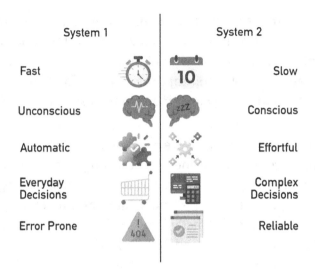

System 1			System 2
Fast			Slow
Unconscious			Conscious
Automatic			Effortful
Everyday Decisions			Complex Decisions
Error Prone			Reliable

Figure 2.   Kahneman's Dual Process Model.

The use of the term 'systems' to describe these dual processes is sensible because, unlike the triune model, it does not assume that any one particular segment of the brain is solely responsible for these processes. Rather, multiple areas of the brain work in concert to facilitate these processes. Neuroscientists have been utilizing brain-imaging technology to identify these areas, and activation of System 1 in the brain has been found to be associated with the release of dopamine, a neurotransmitter that influences motivation for rewarding stimuli, pleasure, and instant gratification. Conversely, when people make analytical, System 2-type decisions, the frontal and parietal cortex in the forebrain are activated. Activity in the frontal cortex has been observed to be especially heightened when we are busy contemplating the future consequences of our current actions.

Activating System 1 in people's brains lead them to be more impatient than while activating System 2, as can be observed in studies showing that people have difficulties delaying gratification and prefer instant rewards. In one study, people were asked to choose either a $20 gift card now or a $30 gift card in two weeks. People often choose $20 right away because for most of us System 1 is activated by default and immediate rewards provide instant gratification. In contrast, when people were made to choose between $20 in four weeks and $30 in six weeks, a greater number opted for $30 in six weeks. Because both choices in the second scenario require people to wait before receiving their rewards, people are making choices while oriented towards a long-term time horizon. In both scenarios, people had to wait two additional weeks for the extra $10, but different rewards were chosen because of the temporal dimension involved. Therefore, unless the prefrontal cortex is activated in analytical scenarios such as long-term decision making, System 1 takes default precedence over System 2. Neuroscientists are continuously studying the brain to see how these multiple systems combine to produce our decisions in different contexts.

System 1 in Negotiation and Other Decision-Making Contexts

These insights on the brain provide a useful framework to understand people's behaviors in organizational settings, including in negotiation. In general, System 1 runs the show until System 2 steps in to regulate. The fact that System 1 reflexes can be difficult to preempt and override suggests that they are important enough for the brain to ensure their occurrence without conscious control, despite their propensity to be a nuisance when they get in the way. Let's consider a few of these quirks in the context of negotiations and other decision-making scenarios:

Loss aversion. People hate to lose. When presented with information that conveys potential gains (e.g., the chance to earn money) or losses (e.g., the risk of losing money), people are more sensitive to the information associated with losses. Indeed, most people prefer winning $50 with certainty rather than taking a risky bet in which they toss a coin to either win $100 or get nothing. Leveraging this insight, product marketers design their sales campaigns to include time-limited offers that emphasize what consumers stand to lose if they do not act fast. As described in a previous chapter, when people were approached and told that there were either 'many disadvantages in using cash instead of ZionCard' (loss frame) or 'many advantages in using ZionCard instead of cash' (gain frame), the loss-framed messages induced higher credit card usage than gain-framed messages, underscoring the effectiveness of triggering loss aversion in persuasion and influence.

Loss aversion makes sense from an evolutionary standpoint. Because our cavemen ancestors lived close to subsistence level, the threat of starvation and other dangers meant that they could not afford to squander precious resources. Those who were more averse to losses were more careful at preventing resource losses and, therefore, more likely to survive and reproduce than those who were not. As descendants of loss-averse humans, this proclivity has been passed on to us and is deeply etched in our System 1 processing, making modern-day humans instinctively vigilant against potential losses. When participants in a brain-imaging study were given the choice to gamble with real money, there was enhanced activity in their brains' reward circuitry as the amount of the reward increased and reduced activity in the same circuitry as the potential losses accrued. The reduced activity in the reward circuitry suppresses the ability to imagine pleasure, decreases the motivation to take risks, and increases the urge for conservative, non-loss options. Losses may also trigger greater activity in brain regions that process emotions, such as the amygdala and anterior insula. Patients with lesions on their amygdala were unable to experience loss aversion, suggesting that the amygdala plays a key role in modulating sensitivity towards losses.

To demonstrate the consequences of loss aversion, Harvard University Professor Max Bazerman regularly conducts a simple but illuminating exercise where a $20 bill is auctioned off to his students. The auction's rules are elementary: The winner pays the amount of the bid and 'wins' the $20 bill while the loser pays the amount of the losing bid. Most students generally drop out at about $16 or $17 — they see a bargain if they win and are willing to pay a nominal amount if they come in second. However, there are always a few students who persist because dropping out means having to pay their last bid. In these cases, the bidding continues beyond $20, which is the point where the winner will pay more than the winning prize is worth to win the auction. The leaders keep bidding because losing is a deeply unattractive option. Likewise, negotiators may remain stuck on a bad deal because they do not want to incur losses in terms of the time and effort invested only to walk away empty-handed from the negotiating table.

Impact of emotions on decision-making. Imagine that you are representing a plaintiff in the mediation of a medical malpractice case. During the discussion with the mediator, your client recounts the distressing surgical experience that caused a problem she must live with for the rest of her life. The mediator is an excellent listener — in fact, after sharing the experience, your client remarks that this is the first time anyone has listened so attentively. The mediator then suggests that this is a good time to craft an offer to the other party. But is it?

A common misconception is that after a full and uninterrupted disclosure of the incident, the issues have been laid out so that rational bargaining can occur. However, the neural networks associated with fear are among the most potent and durable across various other human experiences. We are hardwired to be gripped by fearful experiences — even relived memories can be just as harrowing — so that we will never repeat them. Activation of the fear network in the brain, even merely through memories, can under-mine the System 2 processing needed for rational analysis. Thus, just after recounting a traumatic event is not the best time to make well thought-out decisions. It may be important for the mediator to know the details of the incident and for the client to tell the whole story, but it is just as important that the client takes a substantial break before being asked to construct an offer or react to concessions.

Fear is just one of the many emotions that have a significant influ-ence on decisions. Even our simplest choices are affected by emo-tions. Doctors have found that patients with brain tumors that hinder the experience of emotions can struggle to make simple decisions like whether to use a blue or black pen, despite their intellectual functioning remaining intact. Because we tend to asso-ciate decision-making with logical System 2 thinking, it often comes as a surprise that the emotions of System 1 play just as important a role, if not more.

Emotions guide us toward actions that the brain instinctively con-siders appropriate. For instance, other negative emotions, such as disgust and sadness, also significantly impact our state of mind and compel us to prevent or avoid situations associated with them in future. In contrast, positive emotions such as joy and pride feel good, which motivate us to approach whatever led to those good feelings. Anger is a unique emotion that is negative and yet approach-oriented, because it makes us want to get back at people who have wronged us.

Negative and positive emotions also make us either narrow or broaden our focus of attention. Since negative emotions typically arise from undesirable circumstances, our attention tends to be narrowly focused on the source of our negative feelings so that we can deal with them. Fear fixates us on escaping the current situation while sadness makes us agonize for long periods over our loss, which can make it rather difficult to concentrate on anything else. Conversely, positive emotions tend to broaden or expand our sphere of attention. Positive emotions are associated with increased levels of the neurotransmitter dopamine in the anterior cingulate, which have been found to improve creative problem-solving. Creativity is enhanced when we are in a positive emotional state, partly because the release of dopamine improves our capacity to contemplate multiple concepts and perspectives simultaneously.

These different emotions play out during negotiations in various ways. Anger is indicative of power and signals an unwillingness to make concessions, which puts the onus on counterparties to offer more if they want to avoid an impasse. Negotiators sometimes communicate anger to make their counterparts concede more, which can be effective unless the negotiator is clearly in a lower position of power. Communicating disappointment can also lead to concessions by the other party, but only if the disappointment causes them to feel guilty. Regret is another interesting emotional experience that may happen when negotiators accept a proposed offer too readily. Also known as the 'winner's curse', a rapid acceptance of an offer may make the proposer feel that they gave up too much value to the other side. Honorable proposers will respect the acceptance, but there are others who cannot get over their regret and rescind their offers in a bid to try and change terms.

Group bias. Humans evolved to live in groups to better survive the challenges of the pre-modern era. One consequence of human group behavior is the tendency to view people as either in-group members (us) or out-group individuals (them). Also termed as a coalitional mentality, this group-oriented psychology contributes to

System 1 biases such as conformity and favoritism toward members of the in-group, as well as fear and hostility toward out-groups.

These biases toward the in-group and against the out-group are hard to suppress. In-group conformity can lead to herd behavior and groupthink, where group members favor harmony and consensus too much and shy away from challenging group decisions or offering vital alternative viewpoints. Famous examples of groupthink include the demise of Swissair due to the executive board's overconfidence in its financial prospects, as well as the US government's failure to anticipate Pearl Harbor, the Bay of Pigs invasion, the Vietnam War escalation, and the Second Gulf War. In these cases, the ideas and directions put forth by group leaders were not adequately contemplated or challenged by others around them.

Out-group hostility escalates when the intergroup situation is made salient, such as during competitions and wars. One famous experiment involving children demonstrated how easily in-group/out-group bias can be triggered. When Jane Elliot, a teacher, arbitrarily profiled her 7-year-old pupils with blue eyes as 'superior' to their brown-eyed classmates, within minutes, the blue-eyed children ridiculed their unfortunate classmates and ostracized them. Elliot then turned the tables and showed that when the brown-eyed children were given power and superiority, they exacted the same punishments onto their blue-eyed classmates. In the context of negotiation, there is an instinctive tendency to view the situation as adversarial. Therefore, it is unsurprising that people often arrive at the negotiating table armed with a coalitional mentality, especially during group negotiations where the intergroup context is more pronounced.

Brain-imaging studies show that individuals with strong group bias displayed activation in two areas of the cortex: the *medial prefrontal cortex* and the *pregenual anterior cingulate cortex*. The first is believed to be associated with social identity, or how we think about positive traits that link us with our social group, which causes us to express more in-group favoritism. The second is associated with integrating information between the limbic system and the prefrontal cortex and for evoking positive or negative emotions, which may facilitate the association of positive feelings with the in-group. In a study involving soccer fans, participants observed fans from the same or rival teams receiving electric shocks and were asked how much they wanted to help with sharing those shocks (so that the persons getting shocked did not have to endure the shocks all the way). Participants were generally willing to share the shocks with fans from their own team and this was associated with activation of the *anterior insula*, which is related to empathy and understanding the predicament of others. In contrast, when participants saw rival fans experiencing pain, they were reluctant to help and this attitude was, rather tellingly, associated with activation of the *nucleus accumbens*, an area associated with the experience of pleasure.

Trust and empathy. As humans have a fundamental need to rely on others within their social or family groups, instincts to detect and build trust are therefore necessary. Trust appears to be driven by the neuropeptide oxytocin and special types of neurons in the brain called *mirror neurons*. Oxytocin plays a key role in attachment and affiliation by increasing the willingness to be trusting in interpersonal interactions within the same community. When participants in a study were given a boost of oxytocin, they became more trusting in games involving risky investments and more generous in games that involved sharing a fixed amount of resources. Some activities naturally increase the production of oxytocin, including teamwork, eating together, or physical touching, which explains the continued relevance of physical contact greetings like handshakes and hugs. Interestingly, this increase in trust due to oxytocin has been found to occur only with in-group members and not with out-group individuals. In fact, increased oxytocin can lead to more defensiveness and hostility toward persons perceived as competitive or outsiders.

This tendency to trust and relate to other in-group members is supported by the activity of mirror neurons. Experiments with monkeys showed that monkeys who watched another person or monkey doing an act had the same brain activity signature as those who actually did the act. This phenomenon was also discovered in humans. For instance, when we see someone drinking a glass of water, our brain registers the scene as if we were actually drinking the water ourselves. These mirror neurons enable us to recognize the emotions of others without being aware of what those emotions are. This mirroring is believed to be the neural mechanism by which the actions, intentions, and emotions of others can be automatically understood by observers. Through this mirroring, we also end up displaying the same emotions and actions of others, such as through our body language and facial expressions, and studies show that people find each other more relatable and likeable when they unknowingly mirror one another. Subsequent experiments have further demonstrated that when people had their faces anesthetized, they found it harder to recognize the facial expressions of others.

These findings highlight the importance of face-to-face negotiations to develop trust and empathy. The advent of online communication technologies has increased our ability to negotiate in cyberspace, but neuroscience warns that when negotiating parties cannot see each other, they will have a harder time determining the intentions of their negotiation counterparts and hesitate to trust their information and offers.

Fairness. The need to live in groups also gives rise to challenges associated with group living, in particular the problem of freeloaders who leech off the group without contributing themselves. Humans are equipped with an instinctive sense of fairness so that unjust and selfish behaviors can be recognized and punished. This sense of fairness can be elicited through the 'ultimatum' game where one player, the proposer, is given a sum of money and is tasked with deciding how to split it with another player, the responder. Once the proposer communicates their decision, the responder may accept or reject the proposed split. If the responder accepts, the money is split as per the proposal and both parties get to keep the money; if the responder rejects, both players receive nothing. Responders refuse offers when the proposer is seen as behaving unreasonably or selfishly. For example, responders overwhelmingly reject a 99:1 split, even though receiving 1% is technically still a net gain for the responder. In fact, various experiments show that responders tend to reject offers where they get less than 30% of the cut. Proposals deemed as fair (typically a 50:50 split) have far higher chances of being accepted.

Brain scans of people playing such games reveal very rapid activation of the anterior insula and areas of the frontal cortex (in milliseconds), faster than the time taken by the brain to make a conscious cognitive decision. Thus, these fairness reactions are due to instinctive responses from System 1 rather than conscious deliberations from System 2. In another experiment, where people observed fair or unfair players receiving electric shocks, the empathy-related neural responses of observers, especially that of men, were significantly reduced when unfair players were shocked but not when fair players were shocked. Therefore, while fair play and cooperation promote feelings of trust and empathy, receiving or even simply observing selfish, uncooperative behavior prompts anger and a desire to punish non-cooperators.

Confirmation bias. The behaviors described so far all derive from human instincts that function to promote safety, security, and survival. Therefore, without having to learn any skills or acquire any knowledge, a human growing up in the wilderness would still come well-equipped with the natural instincts to avoid losses, react from emotions and favor their in-group. There is yet another kind of bias that differs from these instincts — the basis of which pertains to knowledge, beliefs, and assumptions rather than survival reflexes. This pertains to *confirmation bias*, or the tendency to pay more attention to information that confirms what we already believe.

By relying on memory associations, pattern-matching, and assumptions, System 1 seeks to quickly create a coherent, plausible story — a rationale for what is happening — above all else. This simple sense-making strategy generally works well for rationalizing commonplace, everyday situations. Since childhood, we absorb information and ideas through experience, building our own internal knowledge base that corresponds more or less with how the world around us works. Over time, these knowledge structures become hardened beliefs and assumptions through which we understand or interpret reality. When we observe something that calls for an explanation, such as when a friend is late for an appointment, we select among various plausible explanations the one that seems most coherent with what we know in order to reach an understanding.

This confirmation process therefore also reinforces what we already assume or believe. If we hold a preexisting belief of the friend as a punctual person, we would rationalize their lateness as probably due to some unintentional and unavoidable hold up. But if the friend has a reputation for being late, then we would attribute the lateness to their character. In both rationalizations, our prior beliefs are reinforced as we opt for the understanding we are most familiar with. Although this serves as an effective mental shortcut in general day-to-day scenarios, it can lead to errors such as biased judgments and incorrect conclusions. The propagation of online falsehoods, for example, occurs precisely because people unwittingly share fake articles and stories that support what they (want to) believe. When we negotiate with a counterpart of a certain ethnic origin, our assumptions can also influence how we interpret their actions, inadvertently causing us to view them in ways that confirm our stereotypes.

What Can Informed Negotiators Do?

Broadly speaking, these various instinctive, reflexive, and biased actions are brought about by System 1 to protect or help us. It does not assume that we know better in most situations and provides us with mental shortcuts to guide us under uncertainty. It also ensures that we default to safety first — avoid risks, be part of the herd — before we can harbor any thoughts of exploiting opportunities. What negotiation insights can we gain from this?

For a start, we will know which negotiation approaches are counterproductive. There is a prevalent idea that one should always present a poker face and suppress emotions during negotiations. Antiquated tactics founded on ideas such as withholding information and zero-sum compromise viewed negotiations through an excessively rational and asocial lens. Thus, old-school negotiation approaches not only disregarded emotions but also treated them as a liability.

On the contrary, neuroscience indicates that emotions and other System 1 instincts drive the decision-making process as much as rational System 2 cognition; in many cases System 2 may not even factor at all. Knowing that emotions play a huge part in helping people make decisions and building trust suggests that we should pay more attention to how we express emotions — putting forth the right ones at the right time. So, try putting aside that poker face and tap into your counterpart's emotional side by expressing sincerity instead. Their mirror neurons will catch on and facilitate the forming of empathy and trust. This will be further compounded by the release of oxytocin once counterparties perceive you as working with them, not against them. Older theories and approaches that overlook the emotional and social side of negotiations forget that negotiations are fundamentally a human social activity. The more negotiators feel like they are interacting with a robotic, unfeeling counterpart, the more they will refuse to budge. As social creatures, we are wired to want to work and cooperate with others, so it is deep in our nature to be more accommodating and giving once trust is built — it even feels good to give more to those we trust and like.

The behavioral economist Dan Ariely elucidates this with a great example of social versus money markets. The invention of money is a relatively new phenomenon in the span of time that humans have existed; we have operated through social markets — the barter trade of goods and the reciprocal exchange of favors — for the most part of our existence. Using a money market mindset when a social market mindset is more relevant is a major *faux pas*. Consider this scenario: One day, your best friend calls and says, "Hey, I need some help moving some furniture." Being best friends, you make the long trip over to his place and spend two hours moving some heavy chairs and tables. After the work is done, your friend calculates the utility of your effort and says, "Thanks for your help, buddy! Here's $65.70."

Most people would find such a gesture strange, if not insulting. The amount might be rationally fair (and acceptable to a hired laborer), but money is not a good way to show appreciation here. Yet, it is not that money markets are inferior to social markets — money markets exist because they *are* indeed more efficient than social markets. However, money markets are more apt as a means to transact among strangers, especially when deep trust has not been built yet, or you do not anticipate dealing with each other regularly in the long run. The more acquainted two individuals become over time, the more they trust each other. As they increasingly enter a social market to deal, they will get what they need from each other through a cycle of obligations, favors, and indebtedness. The more they engage in this socially driven cycle, the more it reinforces their bonds. Negotiation outcomes can likewise be optimized often far beyond the initial prospects of the intended negotiation when the process emphasizes social rather than strictly rational dynamics.

Being more cognizant of System 1 processes also opens more avenues for effective deal-making. For instance, knowing that people are wired to be averse to losses allows us to tailor our negotiation approach accordingly. By framing an offer in terms of what a negotiating counterpart stands to lose, their loss aversion can be exploited so that the offer becomes more persuasive. On the other hand, and perhaps more importantly, we can also be prepared if counterparts carry a defensive mentality. Framing the negotiation as a mutual effort to reach win–win outcomes can help counterparts move away from a loss-avoidance mindset and open more avenues for creative deals.

Some self-awareness of our own loss aversion can likewise prevent us from becoming too engrossed with what we stand to lose and getting ensnared in suboptimal negotiation outcomes. Although loss aversion appears subject to hardwired brain activity, researchers *do* find that people display varying degrees of neural activity in response to loss aversion, and these wide-ranging neural responses are associated with differences in behavior. For instance, people with less neural sensitivity to both losses and gains are less guarded, less conservative, and more open to risks or opportunities. Being obsessed with avoiding losses is also antithetical to feeling positive, so one can also inoculate against loss aversion by amping up on positivity. Through increased dopamine levels, feeling positive allows the mind to consider a broader scope of ideas and perspectives, thereby fostering the out-of-the-box thinking needed for optimizing deals. Likewise, other strongly rooted emotions can also be dampened by having a conscious appraisal of the emotion and modification through deliberate behavior.

Although much has been said about the difficulty of disengaging from the automaticity of System 1, we can also train ourselves to consciously engage System 2 thinking and disrupt System 1 processes when it is strategic to do so. The ability to regulate our emotions can be honed and reflects the amazing plasticity of the brain. Negotiation outcomes can be vastly improved when all parties move from a competitive, coalitional, win-lose mentality, toward a mindset that can identify benefits for as many participants as possible at the negotiating table.

Chapter 12

BUILDING ORGANIZATIONAL NEGOTIATION CAPABILITIES

The value of negotiation, unfortunately, has not yet been fully recognized as a critical value-creating task. In many cases it remains a discrete, unstructured, and improvised event. Just as individuals without medical or legal education and training would never be allowed to take care of your health or legal issues, why are untrained negotiators allowed to negotiate multi-million-dollar deals? The simple answer is that negotiation, one of our most frequent tasks in life, is de-valued.

High-performing organizations such as Apple and Google are models of success because they invest in recruiting and developing talented individuals and also create a work environment that is designed to support the performance of individuals. They foster a mindset that recognizes that work environments either support or hinder an individual's success at the negotiation task. Interestingly, Israeli policy-makers recognized, more than 40 years ago, that innovation flourishes only in an environment that supports entrepreneurs' innovative ideas. Therefore, it started a $100 million innovation fund that was later privatized. Today, Israel, known as a startup nation, is a global innovator in agricultural sciences, water purification management, and information technology. The Israeli model of creating an entrepreneurship ecosystem is being followed by many countries, including Singapore.

Organizations can create more value by rethinking the negotiation task and investing in building negotiation capabilities at the individual (micro) and the organizational (macro) levels. On the individual level, we already described in detail the cognitive, emotional, relational, and cultural capitals that negotiators should develop (see Chapter 1). Similarly, on the organizational level, investment should be made in creating a *negotiation ecosystem*, which includes norms, structures, and processes that are designed specifically to support the performance of negotiators.

Specifically, such an ecosystem would include the following: strong and continuous support from senior management that would make negotiation a core capability, an organizational culture that promotes and celebrates negotiation excellence as a core capability, a well-designed reward system that rewards negotiators for making only the right deals, a clearly defined performance evaluation system that is based on measurable indicators, a set of efficient negotiation-specific processes, a system that links between deal-makers and deal-implementers, a set of policies and procedures that facilitate negotiators' performance, a core unit of specialized negotiators, a research unit that is responsible for supporting negotiators, a negotiation information system that records and analyzes negotiation events and negotiators' experience, and a company-wide closed negotiation portal to facilitate internal communications between negotiators.

We conclude the chapter with describing briefly the four-stage evolution process for developing negotiation capabilities, and suggest how to reach the core competency level.

Building a Negotiation Ecosystem

Management support. Currently, a key impediment to making negotiation a core competency is insufficient support from senior executives who fail to champion negotiation excellence. Most senior executives focus only on what appears on their radar screen. Once a particular idea or practice appears in the collective consciousness, a widespread process of imitation begins. For example, product quality has always been important, but it was an aspect that was neglected by many companies in the late 1970s. After Japanese companies made product quality a strategic competitive advantage by using the *quality circles* methodology, countless American companies started to imitate by adopting this methodology and other variations such as *six-sigma*. Similarly, evidence-based management, for example, has always been deemed important but not widely-used. Once the *scorecard method* was introduced as an organizational practice, many organizations adopted it.

Excellence in negotiation has not yet gained enough momentum to appear on the managerial radar screen. Perhaps, when executives realize that most negotiators are not as good as they think they are, they will view negotiation as a great source of potential value-creation. Imagine a large organization that transacts a value of $500 million buying or selling products or services. An improvement of organizational negotiation capabilities by only 1% will create a saving of $5 million. It is not difficult to improve negotiation capabilities by 1%. Further imagine if there is an improvement of 5%, in which case the cost-savings would be $25 million. Once executives recognize this value-creation potential, the requirement for negotiation capabilities to become a core competency will be obvious to all.

Culture of excellence. Similar to a culture of excellence in product quality or in innovation, a culture of excellence in negotiation, championed by senior executives, is propagated by shared values, success stories, and celebratory rituals that reinforce successful negotiations. Recently in a negotiation workshop, the first author witnessed how a group of cynical managers shared stories about the organization's incompetence in deal-making. Specifically, the stories centered on poor performance in acquiring companies that failed to create value. The message was clear from the conversation of the managers: the organization as a whole was unable to negotiate value-creating deals.

Organizations that do not emphasize negotiation capabilities can borrow ideas and principles from cultures of excellence in entrepreneurship or innovation. For example, Steve Jobs, the late co-founder of Apple Computers, was the embodiment of innovation. He relentlessly promoted his remarkable passion for developing innovative products that are uniquely designed. Similarly, the founders of Google, Larry Page and Sergey Brin, have been promoting a culture of innovation by encouraging risk-taking and legitimizing failure as an integral part of the innovation process. Uniquely to Google, Google's employees are allowed to use 20% of their working time engaging in tasks that are not necessarily directly related to their daily activities because executives at Google believe that innovation springs from slack time and not from the daily grind. These examples illustrate how support from senior executives can promote a supportive culture. A culture of negotiation excellence should first and foremost promote relentless mastery of the art and science of negotiation; support only value-creating deals and publicly recognize excellent negotiators through awards and other incentives.

Reward system. There is a difference between doing deals and doing the *right deals*. Robert Kohlhepp, the vice-chairman and former CEO of Cintas, a supplier of uniforms, observed that the negotiators in mergers and acquisitions, for example, are evaluated on how many deals they seal and not the future value of these deals. Similarly, senior executives are also motivated by deal completion because they are paid bonuses for closing deals. For example, following the acquisition of Guidant by Boston Scientific in 2006, Boston Scientific executives received a special bonus of $1.98 million in cash plus options and deferred stocks. These benefits were not contingent on the future value that this acquisition might create in five or ten years.

Rewarding deal-makers merely for closing deals, some experts suggest, offers a perverse incentive to undertake deals that may instead destroy value. Self-interested agents, such as investment bankers or real estate brokers, who are compensated only for closing deals, may recommend closing deals even when they should not. For example, Prudential-Bache, an investment firm, recommended that Rawson Food Services, a major supermarket chain in Florida, acquire 43 supermarkets from Pantry Pride Enterprise. Rawson accepted the recommendation and paid Prudential-Bache millions of dollars in advising fees, but, unfortunately, had to file for bankruptcy shortly afterwards. This was a deal that should not have been made. Rawson sued Prudential-Bache and was awarded approximately $26 million by a Florida jury. Given the current skewed nature of the incentives of negotiation, organizations should instead develop a well-designed system that rewards negotiators or agents for closing deals that create both short-term and long-term value.

Performance-based metrics. What is success in negotiation? In general, there are three criteria: the outcomes of the deal are good, the negotiation process is efficient, and the negotiators are satisfied with the way they conducted the negotiation. These general criteria, however, should be "translated" into specific measurable indicators. At Hewlett-Packard, for example, success is defined by measures in four categories: financial (cost reduction), operational excellence (contract cycle time and total cost of negotiation), risk management (reducing legal exposure and risks), and good relationships with counterparties (suppliers, manufacturers, etc.).

Prior to each negotiating event, the success criteria and measurable indicators (metrics) must be defined. The list of measures below are only an example of some possible measures.

1. Measures related to the negotiator's behavior before and during the negotiation: For example, measures related to planning and preparation. More specifically, identifying interests, stating clearly the 'must have' and the 'like to have' objectives, identifying alternatives, developing possible scenarios, and listing creative deal-design options.

2. Measures related to the negotiation process itself: For example, the duration of the negotiation cycle from beginning to end for different types of deals and the average costs of each type of a deal, including personnel, travel, and accommodation costs, associated with negotiating the contracts. The costs should be measured both in total and as a percentage of the deal amount.

3. Measures related to the negotiation outcome: For example, the ratio of the target value to the actually achieved value of each deal, the average price of the deal over a given period, the conversion ratio of deal leads, the net value of the deal and type of deals, and outcome-based ranking between negotiators.

Efficient processes. The outcomes of negotiation depend on many factors including the extent to which the negotiation process is efficient. Hewlett Packard's contract negotiation process, for example, was previously long and troublesome, involving two-stages of negotiation. It was only after procurement officers completed the first stage of negotiation, which focused mainly on price, that senior legal staff could begin the second stage, which focused on the legal issues. Frustrated by this double-track and motivated to create a more efficient and streamlined process, Hewlett-Packard created a Global Contracts team, in which legal experts worked together with procurement officers in a single-step negotiation process.

In organizations, there are many processes that are highly structured. For example, the production process in many factories is structured. Since negotiations are conducted between human beings, negotiation processes should be semi-structured and tailored to fit specific negotiation cases. Semi-structured implies that there are certain tasks that can be structured in advance such as planning templates. Other tasks such as negotiating the specific agenda or the number of negotiators in team negotiation can be then subject to negotiation in the moment. At Nestle, for example, the acquisition deal-making process is structured with a standard template to ensure that key aspects of a deal are covered. However, the standard template serves as a stimulant rather than an impediment. This semi-structured process is flexible enough to allow for adjustments to the particulars of a given negotiation. It is not treated as sacrosanct. Organizations, therefore, should periodically review their negotiation processes and examine the degree to which they are structured, flexible, and efficient.

Deal-creation and deal-implementation. A negotiated deal is no more than an exchange of promises between negotiators which is codified in a legal agreement. Once a deal is signed, the negotiators who have their own goals to achieve move on to the next deal, leaving the implementation to others who also have compelling goals to achieve. Eager to close deals, deal-makers at times do not fully consider issues related to implementing the deal and often create 'implementation problems'. Therefore, as a rule, deal-making and implementation should not be divorced from one another. For instance, when Nestle is interested in acquiring a particular company, the operations people are involved early on in the acquisition process, participating in the evaluation phase of a potential acquisition target. Closing a deal is only half the story. To avoid a disconnect between deal formulators and implementers, they must work together whether at the negotiation table or away from it.

Policies and procedures. Concerned with control, organizations tend to centralize and standardize their activities by developing uniform policies and procedures across divisions, product lines, and geographic locations. Sometimes, however, they ignore the specific needs and demands of customers or suppliers in certain segments of the market or geographic areas. For example, a multi-billion-dollar company issued a new global pricing policy for selling its commodities. The prices of the different commodities are transparent, indexed (subject to fluctuations), and not discounted. Global pricing, as it turned out, worked well with European buyers. However, Asian buyers disliked this policy and still insisted on negotiating discounts, i.e., lower prices. The notion of a global fixed-price is still foreign in India and China. Not surprisingly, the companies' salespeople found it extremely difficult to deal with Indian and Chinese buyers. To be more responsive to negotiations in different markets, geographical locations, or cultures, organizations should periodically conduct a *fitness-test* in order to examine the extent to which their policies and procedures fit the negotiation context, and check whether they support or hinder the performance of their negotiators.

Core negotiating team. Recognizing the value of having a strong in-house negotiation capability, Nestle established a core team of experienced deal-makers who are involved in every large-scale deal. Similarly, paramilitary organizations clearly recognize the importance of crisis negotiation and often establish *crisis negotiation units* staffed with in-house expert negotiators. In contrast, many multi-national organizations have failed to create national or global core teams of negotiators. For example, a global consumer product company that has more than 4,000 retail outlets around the world delegates the task of negotiating multi-million-dollar deals for commercial real-estate leases to the respective country managers. Some country managers may be skilled in negotiating commercial real-estate leases; however, many are likely not. Given the financial scope (hundreds of millions of dollars) of these negotiations, such large-scale organizations could certainly benefit from establishing a core unit of first-class negotiators who will work closely with the negotiators on the ground — country managers, procurement personnel, salespeople, or business developers — in order to create superior outcomes.

Research unit. In a recent survey, 250 global executives involved in mergers and acquisitions admitted that there were breakdowns in their due-diligence processes such that important deal-related issues were not detected. In contrast to this case, the findings of a study of 1,700 mergers show that in the highest performing mergers, executives conducted more effective due-diligence research, including superior investigations and analyses.

The value of sound research is self-evident. Unfortunately, many negotiators fail in this task for three main reasons. Firstly, busy negotiators do not always have the time to do the necessary research in order to prepare and plan well. Secondly, many negotiators are not familiar with sophisticated and systematic preparation and planning frameworks. Thirdly, many organizations do not provide their negotiators with easy-to-use templates — structured documents on how to research, prepare, or plan well.

Interestingly, some hedge-fund managers, who do not underestimate the value of research and the power of good information, hire former Israeli Mossad (espionage organization) operatives and Central Intelligence Agency (CIA) agents to collect legally available information from public sources. Whether organizations hire due-diligence firms to do necessary research or tackle it in-house, they must recognize the value of information. Most negotiators should not spend their valuable time collecting data, instead getting good information directly from a dedicated team of researchers who are skilled in doing research.

Negotiation information system. Business intelligence and data-mining are common in marketing and in supply chain management. Many organizations invest enormous resources in collecting and analyzing external and internal data in order to make well-informed business decisions. Furthermore, in organizations that value learning from experience, individuals complete structured *after-action reports*, which are carefully analyzed and the lessons that are learned therein are implemented. This is, however, not the case when it comes to negotiation and learning from past negotiations because negotiation events are not 'captured', i.e. recorded or analyzed.

The purpose of establishing a negotiation information system is to facilitate the recording, storage, and analysis of all negotiation events and experiences of the negotiators. This negotiation database should be designed and uniquely structured by each organization based on their own unique characteristics and needs. However, there should be a template of the generic elements: the negotiation context, purpose of the negotiation, the profile of all the negotiators, issues and interests of the parties, deal-design options, possible alternatives, including BATNA, strategic implications if there is no-deal, negotiation process, outcomes, lessons learned, and implications for future negotiations.

Negotiation portal. The purpose of the virtual and closed negotiation portal is to create a secured platform for negotiators in the same organization to network. The portal will effectively facilitate an on-going internal learning community of deal-makers. Hewlett-Packard, for example, created the *Negotiator's Garage*, an online negotiation resource library that includes training resources, templates for plan-ning and preparation, stories of negotiation histories, and much more. Other organizations can similarly benefit from a negotiation portal uniquely designed for their needs that includes training con-tent, industry specific articles related to deal making, tailor-made templates, chat rooms for consultation, and discussion boards.

The Stages of Organizational Negotiation Capabilities

As stated earlier, developing competitive capabilities in innovation, product quality, customer service, or supply chain management take time. It begins first and foremost with a deliberate managerial deci-sion to elevate a particular task to the level of a strategic thrust and allocate the necessary resources to it. To make negotiation an impor-tant organizational capability requires both intent and resources. Whereas in some organizations, neither managerial attention nor resources are allocated to building negotiation capabilities, in other organizations it is the opposite. Below we describe briefly a four-stage evolution process of negotiation capabilities within an organization:

- **Ground Zero:** Organizations at the *ground zero* stage do not recognize the negotiation task as one that can create any value and thus do not invest any resources in building either individual or organizational capabilities. They do not provide either inter-nal or external training in negotiation. In addition, attention is not paid to building norms, processes, or structures that sup-port the negotiators' performance. Many organizations are at the *ground zero* stage.

- **Embryonic:** Organizations at the *embryonic* stage see negotiation as a somewhat important skill to have, but exclusively for a small select group of professionals, typically, sales and procurement personnel. These organizations encourage the select group with direct negotiation responsibilities to attend short-term training offered by commercial training companies or universities. However, the training in many cases is not comprehensive enough. In almost all these cases, the training programs do not include a systematic follow-up regarding application of the learning or one-on-one coaching. In addition, organizations in the *embryonic* stage also do not have in place a negotiation ecosystem — a set of norms, processes, and structures to support their negotiators' performance.
- **Growth:** Organizations at the *growth* stage recognize negotiation as an important capability and offer training in negotiation to professionals in a variety of sales, marketing, procurement, contracting, public-relations, human resources, legal, and managerial roles. Given the scale and cost of the training, it is typically offered internally by either internal or external trainers. For example, Accor, the world's leading hotel operator and market leader in Europe, offers training conducted by internal and external trainers. Organizations at the *growth* stage invest significant resources in training. However, post-training implementation, mentoring, and coaching are limited to a few high-performers identified as those with high potential. These individuals are typically assigned a mentor or a coach. At this stage, the focus is still exclusively on building individuals' negotiation capabilities and not on building organizational-wide negotiation capability.
- **Core competency:** Senior executives at the *core competency* stage clearly recognize the significant value of the negotiation task and thus allocate significant resources to making it a source of competitive advantage by focusing on the individual and the organizational levels. On the individual level, training in basic and

advanced negotiation is offered not just to those who negotiate directly with customers or suppliers, but to most employees of the organization. The training is designed to develop individuals' tactical and strategic capability in negotiation and influence. The assumption is that individuals who are skilled at negotiation and influence will be effective in their interactions with internal as well as external stakeholders. The training at this level, however, should be more comprehensive and include the aforementioned four capitals and also offer mentoring opportunities either by internal or external experts in negotiation. On the organizational level, organizations at the *core competency* stage invest heavily in building a *negotiation ecosystem* — a set of norms, processes, and structures that are designed to support the negotiators' performance across the organization.

Starting Out

The process of building individual and organizational negotiation competencies is long and requires significant resources. Below are general suggestions:

1. **Negotiators' audit:** The purpose of this audit is to assess the current level of the negotiators' four capitals. Specifically, to assess their negotiation knowledge, skills, and attitude related to cognitive, emotional, relational, and cultural capitals. Based on this audit, it will be later possible to determine the negotiators' capabilities gap.
2. **Organization's audit:** The purpose of this audit is to assess the current state of the organization's negotiation ecosystem. More specifically, to assess the extent to which the current organizational norms, processes, and structures support the negotiators' performance. Based on this audit, it will be later possible to identify the gaps in the organization's ecosystem.
3. **Management commitment:** Following an assessment of the current state of the negotiators' capitals and negotiation

ecosystem, senior management has to make a deep commitment to building both.

4. **Developing negotiators' capitals:** In most negotiation courses, seminars, and workshops, the primary focus is on building cognitive capital. Typically, the emphasis is on learning how to apply a planning framework, understanding the principles of persuasion and how to use them, mapping the stakeholders and identifying their interests, or doing a power relations analysis. Not enough attention, however, is given to managing emotions intelligently, fostering and developing relationships and trust, or developing cultural awareness and sensitivity. A solid training program must be experiential and focus on developing cognitive, emotional, relational, and cultural knowledge and skills that are related specifically to negotiation. While providing comprehensive training is necessary, it is however not sufficient. It should be supplemented by one-on-one coaching and mentoring.

5. **Developing an organization's ecosystem:** Based on an in-depth organizational audit and assessment of the gap between the current state of the negotiation ecosystem and the desired level, serious considerations must be given to developing the necessary organizational norms, processes, and structures. For example, designing a context-specific performance metrics and reward system, or establishing a negotiation information system.

Printed in the United States
by Baker & Taylor Publisher Services